Bishops' Conference of England & Wales

LIVING + SHARING
OUR FAITH

A NATIONAL PROJECT OF CATECHESIS
AND RELIGIOUS EDUCATION

"To live is to change"

A way of reading Vatican II

Christopher Jamison OSB

Damian Lundy FSC

Louisa Poole SSL

Published with the authority of the
Department for Catholic Education and Formation
Bishops' Conference of England and Wales

Rejoice Publications

Living and Sharing Our Faith
A National Project Publication

Published by
Rejoice Publications
19 Wellington Close
Chelmsford, Essex CM1 2EE

Distributed by
Matthew James Publishing Ltd,
P.O. Box 2305
Chelmsford, Essex CM1 2HU

ISBN 1 899481 07 9
First published 1995
© 1995 Department for Catholic
Education and Formation Bishops'
Conference of England & Wales

Nihil obstat:
Fr Anton Cowan, *Censor*
Imprimatur:
Monsignor Ralph Brown, V.G.
Westminster, 17th October, 1994

Design: *Jeff Carter*
Calligraphy: *Ewan Clayton*
Cover Design: *Jeff Carter*
Printed by: *4edge Ltd, Hockley*

Acknowledgements

Quotations from the documents of the Second Vatican Council used in this text are taken from the translation of **Decrees of the Ecumenical Councils**, volume II, edited by Norman Tanner, SJ, *Sheed and Ward*, 1990, and are used by permission of the publishers.

Photo credits

Collages

p.8: medallions clockwise from top 1, *The Universe*; 2,3,4,6,9 © Neil Beer; 7 © David Parry; 8 © Des Brennan; reflections © Joe Coughlan; global view, atomic cloud © fsp-Rome;

p.28: Left: top, centre © St Paul Multimedia UK; bottom © Lawrie Law; Centre: top, centre, bottom courtesy of Des Brennan; Right: top, bottom © Neil Beer, centre Des Brennan;

Other

p.7 portrait of J.H. Newman by courtesy of Sisters of St. Louis, Newmarket; pp 10,83 courtesy of *The Universe*; p34 courtesy of Worth Abbey, Sussex; pp 27,66,75 courtesy of Bushey parish, Herts; p.76 courtesy of De La Salle Brothers; p.86 bottom courtesy of Carmelites, Quiddenham.

Neil Beer © pp.16 (11 photos), 26 top,49,54,58,62,91,94,100 top,111,122 centre,128,132,133; Süd Verlag p104; AFP France p122 top; fsp-Rome pp106,107; St Paul Multimedia UK © pp.16 bus queue,26 bottom,100 bottom,122 bottom; Andes Press Agency © p57; Joe Coughlan © pp.65,112; Marie Gurhy © p.44;

Contents

Acknowledgements

The gratitude of the authors goes to the many people who have helped us to realise that 'to live is to change', during the years of preparation and revision of this study.

The work was begun by parishioners of the Sacred Heart and St John the Evangelist, Bushey, Hertfordshire, who produced the first draft summaries of the Council documents as part of their adult education programme. We want to thank Father Guy Sawyer, parish priest, Peter Keenan, Bernard Amos and more than fifty members of the Bushey parish, who began and supported this study from their love of the Church, their desire to grow in awareness of its mission in the world, and their wish to share their knowledge and enthusiasm with others.

We thank the following religious communities: the Sisters of St Louis in Harringay, the De La Salle Brothers in Kensington and Oxford, the Benedictines of Worth, and the Sacred Heart Community at St Albans. They supported us and our project with continual interest and encouragement, as well as with unstinted hospitality, care and facilities.

We also acknowledge the help of the staff of the Catholic Central Library and their resources; the Steering Committee of the National Project and, in particular, Anne White, co-ordinator of the Project, who was our tireless adviser and counsellor in the later stages of our journey.

The penultimate draft of this book was read by many bishops, diocesan Religious Education advisers, teachers, college and seminary lecturers, who offered much detailed and helpful advice. We are grateful for their interest and support, and we have incorporated many of their suggestions into the final version of our text. Our intention was always to produce a document for discussion, not a text which claims to be an authoritative substitute for the documents of the Council. We offer the fruits of our research as a contribution to the development of adult Christian education in the Church and the world.

Christopher Jamison OSB
Damian Lundy FSC
Louisa Poole SSL

Foreword

To Live is to Change is a challenging title, and it is only when we cease to recognise this challenge that we drift and fail to respond to Christ's call to us to share in the life and mission he has given to his Church. For the Church is something we share in all the time, not a distant duty, calling for mere attendance and support.

The Second Vatican Council was a powerful call for renewal, for our spiritual, liturgical, social and political enlivenment. It was the occasion of new insights and understanding of the nature of the Church, of shared responsibility, of true relationships between distinct ministries, of equality of dignity of all in the sight of God, and of the need to reach out with the Good News of the Gospel towards those bewildered or misled in a self-centred world.

We have all come through an immense time of development, when the temptation has been to settle for confrontational categories and titles, rather than open our hearts to a great stirring of the Holy Spirit.

As the last bishop in England and Wales, not yet in retirement, who was one of the Council Fathers and shared in the preparation of the Council documents, I realise that is now thirty years behind us and we must not think that its products were the last word. There are already signs of the need for further developments as our technological world judders its way forward. But if we are to face more change, it is necessary that today's generations absorb the true lessons of Vatican II, in light of the Synods which have followed, and now often clarified in the new Catechism of the Catholic Church.

In this process the National Project of Catechesis and Religious Education has a major part to play. This study of the teachings of Vatican II, though not pretending to be comprehensive, is a valuable aid in the rich tapestry of material now available for use in our schools, colleges and parishes. My hope must be that this publication, valuable in itself, will inspire some of its readers to study more deeply the issues it raises and about which it gives good guidance. It professes to be no more than *a* way of reading Vatican II. It is indeed a valuable arrangement of material but not just for academic study. It is an aid to the enlivenment for which in our time the Spirit has called.

✝ Derek Worlock
Archbishop of Liverpool

Introduction

This book aims to answer one simple question: **'What is Vatican II?'**

Even a simple answer would have to acknowledge that Vatican II was a momentous occasion, a turning-point in the life of the Catholic community, a great gathering in the 1960s where the Catholic Church sought new ways of being a more effective Christian community in the modern world. The process continues to this day. That is why the question reads: 'What **is** Vatican II?' not just 'What was Vatican II?'

Aspects of Vatican II were, and are, controversial. The authors of this book are enthusiastic about the Council and about the changes it sought to introduce into the life of the Church. We ask readers to bear in mind that our account of the historical process which preceded the Council is necessarily condensed. The Catholic Church before and after Vatican II is the same Church, although there are contrasts between Catholic life prior to 1962 and since the Council. In our enthusiasm about many of the changes introduced into the life of the Church by and since Vatican II, we do not wish to caricature the beliefs and practices of a previous generation. We invite our readers to enter into a dialogue with us, and to ask lots of questions about the Church. The aim of the dialogue is to help us all to be with the Church on its pilgrim journey. As the Council said,

> 'In its pilgrimage on earth, Christ summons the Church to continual reformation, of which it is always in need, in so far as it is an institution of human beings here on earth.' (*Decree on Ecumenism* 6)

Thirty years on, however, there is still uncertainty as to what Vatican II is all about. Take, for example, the following dialogue from the movie *Nuns on the Run*:

[Robbie Coltrane is tucking into a plate of sausages and bacon.]

Eric Idle: *"How come you're a Catholic and you're eating meat on Friday?"*

Robbie Coltrane: *"Agh, that's all changed since Vatican II!"*

Eric Idle: *"Vatican II? What's that? Deputy Pope?"*

Not only in movies but in real life, not only among those outside the Church but also among Catholics, people are still asking: 'What is Vatican II?' Clearly, our simple question requires something more than a simple answer.

OUR LINE OF APPROACH

This book aims to answer the question 'What is Vatican II?' by inviting the reader to enter into the process begun by the Council. The book is in two parts.

Part One describes the process by which Vatican II emerged, how it arrived at its conclusions, and the impact these have had. This part is called *Towards the Making of the Modern Church*.

Part Two contains a description and an analysis of the documents published by the Council. This part is called *Towards an Understanding of Vatican II*.

The modern world is characterised by rapid change. Without losing its deep roots in the unchanging Word of God, the Church too is a community that grows and changes. One prophetic figure who understood the nature of change in the Church was Cardinal Newman. In 1845 he wrote: 'To live is to change and to be perfect is to have changed often' (*The Development of Christian Doctrine*). From his words are taken the title of this book. The Catholic Church is still growing, still changing, still striving to realise the vision of Vatican II.

USING THIS BOOK

This book may be useful for those who are examining the Second Vatican Council as part of a Religious Studies programme. The authors hope that it will also be of wider interest within Catholic or ecumenical groups. It also provides helpful background and further resources for anyone using or reading the new *Catechism of the Catholic Church*. It is interesting to note that in that publication, the greatest number of quotations and references, after the Scriptures, come from the documents of Vatican II.

We suggest two ways for using this book in a parish group:

1. You could read it in the order in which it is presented or you could follow your own area of interest, using the questions offered throughout the text and discussing your reactions. For instance, the parishioners in Bushey who started this project were very enthusiastic about the *Declaration on Religious Freedom*.

2. You may find it rewarding to share your experiences with others in a group, remembering the Lord's words: 'Where two or three are gathered in my name, I am there among them". (For a process to use see p. 27)

John Henry Newman
1801-1890

'the hidden father of the Council'

John Henry Newman was an Anglican cleric and scholar. After forty years as an Anglican, his convictions about the authority of the Roman Catholic Church led him to become a Roman Catholic, but he never lost his respect for Anglicanism. In 1879 he was named a Cardinal.

At a time when clergy often wanted laity to keep out of church affairs, he insisted that lay people were central to the Church's life, commenting wryly that 'the Church would look foolish without them'.

He studied modern ideas, accepting evolution and scientific bible study, provided they left God in place. His Essay on the Development of Christian Doctrine (1845) showed that doctrine is always developing in order to express itself in new circumstances; development is the way doctrine preserves itself. This view was almost unheard of among Catholic theologians at that time, who tended to think that the way to preserve doctrine was to prevent development. So Newman was the prophet of Christian unity, of the laity, of religious education, of returning to the sources in order to develop new ways of expressing faith.

The People of God…
a most sure seed of unity, hope and salvation
for the whole human race.
Lumen Gentium, 9

The Great Questions

The origins of our modern world lie not so much in a new set of answers as in a new set of questions. So we must begin by examining those questions.

Charles Darwin caused a sensation when he published his book *On the Origin of Species* in 1859. He suggested that the human race was descended from the apes by a random process called natural selection. This suggestion raised the first great modern question: 'What is a human being?'

Since Darwin, there have been many answers. Some think that we are indeed just naked apes. Others have proposed that we are participants in the revolutionary struggle towards the communist state. Some are engaged in establishing the superiority of one race or gender. Others again believe that we are individuals who should 'do our own thing'.

The Church had always had a clear answer to the question: human beings have their origin in God and are called to live in the Spirit of Christ. But other people's answers challenged the Church's answer, and indeed challenged the Church's right to exist at all. During the twentieth century, secularism became widespread. Secularism is the tendency in modern society to live without reference to God or religion. This raised a second great modern question: 'What is the Church?' or perhaps 'What is the Church for?'

In previous ages, the Church had summoned Councils to face questions about the identity of Christ and other matters of faith. The Church in our day summoned a Council to face these two great modern questions:

What is a human being?

What is the Church?

Pope John XXIII called the Second Vatican Council to meet in 1962. Nearly a hundred years before, the Church had already started to face these questions at the first Vatican Council, but the task was left unfinished. The story of the Second Vatican Council, therefore, must begin with the unfinished business of this earlier Council.

A way to begin to understand the process begun by the Council is to understand the process of the modern world itself.

Darwin's dilemma

Writing to a friend, Darwin spoke of...

'the extreme difficulty or rather impossibility of conceiving this immense and wonderful universe as the result of blind chance. When thus reflecting, I feel compelled to look to a First Cause and I deserve to be called a Theist. But then arises the doubt – can the mind of man, which has, as I fully believe, been developed from a mind as low as that possessed by the lowest animals, be trusted when it draws such grand conclusions?'

John 23 = VC II

9

what is a council of the church?

A Council of the Church is known as a general or ecumenical council. It consists of all the bishops of the Catholic Church throughout the world.

The authority of a Council united with the Pope is supreme in the Church. The authority of the Pope himself was defined at Vatican I.

The purpose of a Council is to decide upon fundamental matters of faith. When the bishops meet, they help each other to find new ways forward. A Council is not an isolated event, however, the whole church carries forward the insights of a Council and works out their implications.

Vatican I

The Unfinished Council

The First Vatican Council (1869-1870) took place against a background of revolutionary turmoil in Europe. The French Revolution had been anti-Catholic in its philosophy and violent in its attacks on Catholic clergy. As the Revolution swept across Europe, the Church became fearful of liberal ideas and of all scientific progress.

Since the Middle Ages, the Pope had been ruler of a sizable country situated in the middle of Italy, a country known as the Papal States. In the nineteenth century, the continued rule of these States by the Pope was considered vital to the independence of the Pope's spiritual leadership. In 1848, Rome itself was caught up in revolutionary turmoil and Pope Pius IX fled the city. France had by now changed its revolutionary government and the current regime thought that the preservation of the Papal States was in France's interest; so in 1849 a French army went to Rome and the Pope was escorted back as ruler.

AN ADEQUATE REMEDY

This experience had a deep effect on Pius IX. He rounded on modern ideas in a series of condemnations. In 1864, he grouped these together and published the *Syllabus of Errors*. The Pope was trying to safeguard the position of the Church against governments and movements that wished to push the Church to one side. To secure the safety of the Church in what was seen as a flood-tide of anti-Catholic forces, Pius IX decided that a Council of the Church was needed. He said its aim was 'to provide an adequate remedy for the disorders, intellectual and moral, of Christendom'. He wanted a Council to confirm his condemnations and to reaffirm the Church's belief in its own divine origin against those who refused to give it any special status.

The Council met in December 1869. Discussions of a long document on the Church dragged on. The political situation in Europe was deteriorating and war was imminent. Many bishops were eager to leave, yet they wished to strengthen the position of the Church. So some bishops introduced for debate a separate, smaller document on the Papacy; they urged the Council to strengthen the Pope's role and to complete discussion of the Church later. After fierce debate, the fourth session of the Council approved the dogmatic constitution on the Pope in July 1870 (*Pastor Aeternus*) .

UNDERSTANDING AUTHORITY IN THE CHURCH

The teaching authority of the Church is based on the doctrine that God keeps the whole Church from false teaching. So, for example, the definitions of Councils of the Church are believed to be free from error. Vatican I reflected on the infallibility of the Church as a whole. The Council applied this infallibility to the Pope as spokesman of the Church when he defines a question of faith or morals. A Pope has only formally exercised this gift once since 1870. This was in 1950, when Pius XII defined the bodily Assumption of Our Lady. As well as defining papal infallibility, Vatican I also defined the Pope's power. The Council said that the Pope can act as the immediate authority over every Catholic, so he can impose discipline on any Catholic person or institution.

The Council seemed to confirm the worst fears of many of the Church's critics. Bismarck, the German Chancellor, launched the *kulturkampf*, a systematic persecution of the Church. Gladstone, the British Prime Minister, declared that no Catholic could now be truly loyal to the Crown. This provoked Newman's famous *Open Letter to the Duke of Norfolk*, in which he pointed out that the new definition was not as extreme as some conservatives had desired. The definition of papal authority did not alter the traditional Catholic teaching that the voice of conscience (correctly understood) must be obeyed as the place where a prudent person can hear the voice of God. Many people, however, interpreted the Council's definition in a strongly centralising way. The Church's principle weapon against liberalism would be the loyalty of its members to the decrees of the Pope. This interpretation was made possible not so much by the definitions as by the suspension of the Council before it could produce a statement on the whole Church.

The discussion of the document on the Church was never completed. War broke out; the Italian Nationalists occupied Rome and the Pope suspended the Council indefinitely.

UNFINISHED BUSINESS

Vatican I left a top-heavy definition of the Church. The aim had been to define the role of the whole Church but all that had been defined was the role of the Pope. One of the first tasks of Vatican II was to put right this imbalance and agree a definition which reintegrated the Pope and the Church. To understand how Vatican II did this, we must examine how the Church's life developed between the two Councils.

ecumenical councils of the church

There have been only 21 ecumenical councils in the history of the Church.

Council	Year	
Nicaea I	325	56
Constantinople I	381	50
Ephesus	431	20
Chalcedon	451	
Constantinople II	553	
Constantinople III	680 - 681	
Nicaea II	787	
Constantinople IV	869 - 870	
Lateran I	1123	
Lateran II	1139	
Lateran III	1179	
Lateran IV	1215	
Lyons I	1245	29
Lyons II	1274	
Vienne	1311 - 1312	> 102
Constance	1414 - 1418	
Florence	1431 - 1445	
Lateran V	1512 - 1517	
Trent	1545 - 1563	> 303
Vatican I	1869 - 1870	
Vatican II	1962 - 1965	> 92

Churches which accept the authority of Councils claim to be Catholic; for example, the Orthodox Church. However, the Orthodox Churches do not accept those Councils that occurred after the great split in 1054 between the Orthodox Churches of the East and the Roman Catholic Church.

11

New Movements in the Church

Pius IX died in 1876 and was succeeded by Pope Leo XIII. He inherited a church that was confident, but whose leading thinkers hesitated to undertake new work. Leo encouraged renewed study of the works of St Thomas Aquinas and initiated a new development of Catholic social teaching. In this new atmosphere, some scholars began to apply scientific methods to religious issues.

In France, Father Alfred Loisy studied the New Testament and the origins of the Church in the light of new archaeological discoveries. In Britain, Father George Tyrrell, a Jesuit, studied dogma and tried to relate it to the religious experience of ordinary people. In Italy, Father Romolo Murri proposed that Catholics should leave behind monarchy and embrace democracy, laying the foundations for the Christian Democrats. When Leo died, however, his successor decided that these developments were going too far too fast and should be stopped.

PIUS X

In 1907, Pius X issued a list of errors to be condemned and explained the dangers of what he called 'Modernism'. Some scholars could not accept this and were excommunicated; such was the fate of Fathers Loisy, Tyrrell and Murri. The suppression of Modernism became a priority for the Church; priests had to swear an anti-modernist oath and vigilance committees were set up in every diocese.

The Modernists had been caught between two ways of arriving at knowledge. Traditionally, people tended to believe what authority told them, but with advances in education, scientific study and technology, people became more inclined only to believe what they had experienced for themselves. To reconcile these two ways of knowing, the Modernists explored religious experience as the foundation of religious faith. This led them to ask new questions about Christian faith and to produce some new answers.

The Church saw their answers as ultimately destructive of faith, and Modernism proved to be a false start in facing these questions. But the questions themselves would not go away. Is biblical criticism acceptable? Is the Church as Jesus intended it to be? Is democracy preferable to monarchy?

12

Constitutions
Decrees
Declarations
Decrees

Resourcement
Return to the sources

influenced Divino Afflante
Spiritu

REVELATION

Most important of all, questions had been raised about the nature of revelation. Church leaders seemed to be saying that God reveals himself to people only through the Church's teaching and through sacraments. Modernists seemed to be saying that God reveals himself through people's personal experience. At the time, the debate seemed to imply a choice between one view or the other. We would now see such a choice as a false opposition. God speaks through both: in the Gospel *and* tradition *and* experience may be heard the voice of God.

BUILDING AND LIVING FAITH

During the twentieth century, the Church slowly realised that it had to do more than condemn the modern world and its questions. Movements grew up that sought to answer the new questions in ways that built on rather than destroyed Catholic faith. For example, the biblical, liturgical and catechetical movements sought to advance the Church's understanding of the Bible, of the liturgy and of religious education. (More will be said about these in Part II.) Through these and other movements, some people were discovering, slowly, new ways of living out Catholic faith in the modern world.

In general, however, the Church was cautious. As Pope from 1939-58, Pius XII continued to condemn the evils of the modern world, especially communism. Yet he also formally approved of the three movements mentioned above. This papal approval enabled research to grow in the period before the Second Vatican Council. This was a vital development, and these movements proved to be the building blocks for Vatican II.

JOHN XXIII

With the election of a new Pope in 1958, an architect had arrived who was not afraid to move the blocks in order to build a modern Church. In 1959 the new Pope, John XXIII, announced that he was summoning the twenty-first Ecumenical Council of the Church. He saw the main aim as *aggiornamento*, which means 'letting in the light of day' or 'renewal'. At the opening of the first session, Pope John declared:

> "The substance of the ancient deposit of faith is one thing, the way in which it is presented is another."

members of the council

Council members included internationally influential bishops like Cardinal Suenens (Belgium), Cardinal Bea (Germany), Bishop Helder Camara (Brazil), Cardinal Lercaro (Italy), Cardinal Alfrink (Holland) and Abbot Butler (England). Ottaviani - everything in regards to doctrine conservative

Advisers like Karl Rahner, Hans Küng, Joseph Ratzinger, Henri de Lubac, Yves Congar, Jean Daniélou, Bernard Häring, John Courtney Murray, Barbara Ward, Charles Davis, Gérard Philips and Joseph Jungman also played a key role in leading forward the bishops in their thinking and in drafting documents. Peritum - lots of libs

Ecumenical 'observers' from other Churches included distinguished academics: Karl Barth, George Lindbeck, also Oscar Cullinan, Anglican Bishop John Moorman and Canon Bernard Pawley.

Motu Proprio
Encyclical
Appostolic Exhortation - comes after synod
Papal Bull

Appostolic Constitution
- Dogmatic Constitutions are Appostolic Constitution that discuss Dogma

The Second Vatican Council (1962-1965)

John XXIII 1881-1963

Angelo Roncalli was born into a family of Italian farm workers. Ordained priest in 1904 he taught theology in the diocesan seminary, and, during the Modernist crisis, was accused of Modernism. From 1925 he was a papal diplomat in Bulgaria, Turkey and Greece which gave him close contact with the Orthodox Churches. In 1944 he was appointed Papal Nuncio in Paris where Archbishop Suhard had declared France to be a dechristianised society and developed new kinds of mission to preach the gospel. In 1953 Roncalli became a Cardinal and Patriarch of Venice.

Elected Pope in 1958 at the age of 77, he knew he was chosen as a caretaker. Yet he seized the opportunity and within three months announced the calling of the Council. His agenda for the Council had been dictated by his life, as he himself noted: 'Those who have lived as long as I have were faced with new tasks in the social order at the start of this century; those who, like me, were twenty years in the East and eight in France, were enabled to compare different cultures and traditions, and know that the moment has come to discern the signs of the times, to seize the opportunity and to look far ahead.'

The Council was to look at the sources of faith and then re-express this faith in the changed circumstances of the modern world. This twin focus is central to understanding the Council. The language and style of the Church before the Council was rooted in a tradition that went back to the Catholic Church's response to the Reformation in the sixteenth century. Now, the Pope was seeking a Catholic way of living that went in two directions at once. Firstly, he wanted a 'return to the sources'; back much further than the sixteenth century, back to the origins of Christianity in the Bible and in the life of the early Church. Secondly, Pope John wanted to look forward, 'reading the signs of the times', to form a Christian understanding of the world in which we live. In doing this, the Pope wanted to pay particular attention to promoting Christian unity. This new focus was to lead to dramatic developments during and after the Council.

PREPARATION AND PROCESS

The method of working required preparatory commissions to be set up which had to produce draft statements on different areas of life for discussion by the Council. During this preparatory period, there were two signs of important new approaches developing.

Firstly, the Secretariat for the Promotion of Christian Unity was set up by Pope John. It invited 40 observers from other churches to attend the Council; this number increased to over 100 during the Council.

Secondly, large numbers of bishops came to Rome from less developed countries. 42% of the bishops were from Latin America, Asia and Africa, seeking new ways of being the Church in their cultures. The theologian Karl Rahner saw it as 'the first act in history where the world Church first began to exist as such'.

There were also striking absences: no laity and no nuns. Eventually, 39 lay men and women and 9 nuns were present as 'listeners'. The Council was the largest ever held, comprising some 2,500 bishops and heads of male religious orders. There were four sessions, one a year from 1962-65. Each session lasted about eight weeks during which drafts from the commissions were discussed and voted on.

Abbot Christopher Butler, one of the Council Fathers from Britain, summed up the way the sessions evolved: "At the beginning of the Council, no one knew which way the Church would renew herself. But by the end of the third session, we realised that it was not going to be a superficial adjustment but a radical one. It meant a radical reappraisal of Catholicism. By then this was not only the view of a progressive minority, but it had captured the centre of the Council."

This process is seen in the way the Council rejected several draft statements and finally, without any draft from a preparatory commission, wrote its own *Pastoral Constitution on the Church in the World of Today*. This was a fitting climax to the process of the whole Council.

If Pope John's Council transformed the Church, his personality transformed the papacy. He was jovial but calm, simple but cultured; he smiled and joked, cared for prisoners and visited parishes. He was a deeply human Pope who wanted to love the world rather than condemn it. In return, the world loved him.

At his last meeting with Pope John, the young Mgr Derek Worlock knelt to receive the Pope's blessing. To his surprise Pope John hauled him to his feet and gave him a bear-hug. After Mgr Worlock, deeply moved, had taken his departure, the Pope then sent his chaplain racing down the corridor after the young monsignor: 'The Pope says, tell that young man that when I embrace someone I mean it'. Looking back on this event, Archbishop Worlock regarded the Pope's words as 'a message to all Churches and all nations'.

A few days before he died, Pope John told one of his staff, "The secret of my ministry is in that crucifix you see opposite my bed. It's there so that I can see it in my first waking moment and before going to sleep...Look at it, see it as I see it. Those open arms have been the programme of my pontificate: they say that Christ died for all, for all. No one is excluded from his love, from his forgiveness."

His life's work is summed up in a comment he made on his death-bed: "It is not that the Gospel has changed; it is that we have begun to understand it better."

Paul VI 1898-1978

Pope John died after the first session of the Council and was succeeded by the Archbishop of Milan, Giovanni Battista Montini. He came from a cultivated and prosperous background and was more reserved than his predecessor. He continued the Council in the same spirit as Pope John, however, and brought it to a successful conclusion.

As the Church implemented the Council's reforms, some said Pope Paul was going too fast, others that he was going too slowly. This caused him considerable personal agony. His commitment to implementing the reforms of the Council was undoubted, a task he carried out with integrity and humility.

Among the difficulties of his pontificate, the greatest was the stormy reception given to his statement 'On Human Life' in 1968, where he affirmed the Church's opposition to artificial contraception. His most publicly acclaimed achievements were statements and visits he made to encourage less developed countries and to promote Christian unity. Outstanding among these were his visit to Latin America and his address to the UN General Assembly; his setting up a commission for Anglican-Roman Catholic dialogue; and his encounter with the Orthodox Patriarch of Constantinople whom he greeted by kissing his feet.

VATICAN II'S
MESSAGE TO HUMANITY

(Here are two extracts from the Council's first statement)

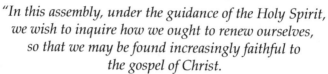

*"In this assembly, under the guidance of the Holy Spirit,
we wish to inquire how we ought to renew ourselves,
so that we may be found increasingly faithful to
the gospel of Christ.
We shall take pains so to present to the people of this age
God's truth in its integrity and purity
that they may understand it and gladly assent to it..."*

*"Coming together in unity from every nation under the sun,
we carry in our hearts
the hardships, the bodily and mental distress, sorrows, longings and hopes
of all the peoples entrusted to us.
We urgently turn our thoughts to all the anxieties by which people today are afflicted.
Hence, let our concern swiftly focus first of all on those
who are especially lowly, poor and weak.
Like Christ, we would have pity on the multitude, weighed down
with hunger, misery and lack of knowledge.
We want to fix a steady gaze on those who still lack
opportune help to achieve a way of life worthy of
human beings."*

In his statement on 'The Progress of Peoples', Pope Paul VI described that new humanism which sums up his own life:

"Even more necessary still is the deep thought and reflection of people in search of a new humanism, one which will enable our contemporaries to enjoy the higher values of love and friendship, of prayer and contemplation, and thus find themselves."

The Council Documents

The original intention of those who planned Vatican II was that the Council's teaching would be presented in some seventy documents. In the end (mercifully, you might think!) only sixteen documents were produced during the four sessions of the Council. Fifteen came from draft documents prepared before the first session began. In some cases these were radically changed during the course of reflection and discussion. The longest document – the *Pastoral Constitution on the Church in the World of Today* - had not been planned in advance. It was conceived and written during the Council itself. Some consider it to be the most important document. Later, we shall see why.

Today most commentators on Vatican II would argue that the most important documents are the **Constitutions**, since they provide the keys to unlocking the basic meaning of the Council. The **Decrees** and **Declarations** depend on the Constitutions and show the practical implications of these for the Church.

OUR ARRANGEMENT OF THE DOCUMENTS

In **Part Two** we offer summaries of the Council documents, accompanied by brief commentaries. The original texts, even when translated from the Latin into modern English, use technical vocabulary and contain subtle distinctions, hammered out in the course of complex debates. Our summaries offer an accurate picture of the message of Vatican II, but do not claim to cover all the detail. This book is no more than an introduction to the Council. It aims to give you a taste of the spirit of Vatican II and to help you realise why its teaching is important for all Christians.

One way of reading the Council's documents is to read them in the order in which they were written or approved. That is not the way we shall follow, for it may make it hard to see the wood for the trees. Our aim is to help you to understand the basic teaching of Vatican II, so we shall examine the documents in four groups to help you see how they fit together into a coherent whole. We invite you to become familiar with this focus and make an introductory tour of the Council's teaching. This will help you to become acquainted with our reading of the main threads of the Council, before the documents are examined in more detail at a later stage.

prayers of the council

Holy Spirit, show once more your wonders in our day as on the day of Pentecost.
(Prayer for the success of the Council)

We are here before you, O Holy Spirit, conscious of our innumerable sins, but united in a special way in your holy Name. Come and abide with us...

May you who are infinite justice, never permit that we be disturbers of justice. Let not our ignorance induce us to evil, nor flattery sway us, nor moral and material interest corrupt us. But unite our hearts to you alone and do it strongly, so that, with the gift of your grace, we may be one in you and may in nothing depart from the truth.
(Prayer of the Council Fathers)

The Documents

FOCUS ON SPIRITUALITY

How do we know God?

How do we relate to God?

What difference does God make to our lives?

The answer to these questions form the basis of what is called 'spirituality' – the way in which we make sense of our lives, our search for meaning, the way in which God saves us and makes us holy. At the centre of a Christian understanding of life is the human relationship with God.

Vatican II's first document *Constitution on the Sacred Liturgy* (SC) presents the Church's understanding of its worship and life of prayer. The later *Constitution on Divine Revelation* (DV), developed in the course of the entire Council, offers a deeper reflection on the relationship of God with believers.

FOCUS ON THE CHURCH

Our personal relationship with God is very important but none of us is saved as an individual. We belong to the community of humankind where no man or woman is an island. Christians belong to the Church of Jesus Christ.

For Catholics the Church is central to our understanding of life: indeed, we *are* the Church. Some people may live a love-hate relationship with the institutional Church. We may find ourselves critical of some practices and customs, and of fellow-members, but the Church is our 'mother', our teacher, our home, our community of faith. Vatican II's central understanding of the Church is that believers are the pilgrim people of God.

The *Constitution on the Church* (LG) presents the fullest, most detailed understanding of the Church ever developed by a Council. The practical application of this theology of the Church (or *ecclesiology*) is offered in five decrees which consider different groups within the people of God:
- baptised lay people, the majority of Church members (AA);
- bishops (CD);
- priests (PO) and those training to be priests (OT); and
- men and women who belong to religious orders (PC).

Other decrees in this group present aspects of the Catholic Church's life and ministry in the 20th century:
- its missionary activity (AG); and
- its ecumenical relationships with other Christian communities (UR).

CELEBRATING OUR RELATIONSHIP WITH GOD

Constitution on the Sacred Liturgy (SC)

Dogmatic Constitution on Divine Revelation (DV)

LIVING AS A COMMUNITY OF BELIEVERS

Dogmatic Constitution on the Church (LG)

Related documents:

Decree on the Apostolate of the Laity (AA)

Decree on the Pastoral Office of Bishops (CD)

Decree on the Ministry and Life of Priests (PO)

Decree on Priestly Formation (OT)

Decree on the Sensitive Renewal of Religious Life (PC)

Decree on Eastern Catholic Churches (OE)

Decree on Ecumenism (UR)

Decree on the Missionary Activity of the Church (AG)

A very important development during and after the Council was a growing sense of the importance of local Churches. This was first worked out in the *Constitution on the Church* (LG) and applied to one group, the Eastern Catholic Churches (OE). In the years following Vatican II the wider implications came to be appreciated; for instance, in the Catholic communities of Latin America whose bishops made a serious attempt to work out the significance of Vatican II for their churches during their conference at Medellin, Colombia, in 1968, and at major conferences which followed. In England and Wales, the implications of the Council for the Catholics in our country began to be worked out at the National Pastoral Congress held in Liverpool in 1980. *The Easter People* is the statement of the bishops, published after the Congress. It expresses the hopes and vision of that gathering of the local Church of England and Wales.

FOCUS ON THE CHURCH IN THE WORLD OF TODAY

When Pope John XXIII decided (in 1959) to call a Council, he made it clear that one of the most important tasks of the Second Vatican Council was to bring the Church up-to-date. (He used the Italian word *aggiornamento* – see p. 13) Indeed the first sentence of Vatican II's first document announces the Council's desire 'to adapt those structures which are subject to change so as better to meet the needs of our time' (SC 1). This is one of the main thrusts of all sixteen documents, and it provides the central emphasis of Vatican II's longest and most complex statement, the *Pastoral Constitution on the Church in the World of Today* (GS).

In this, the Council, relying on the inspiration of Christ, 'proposes to elucidate the mystery of humankind and, in addressing all people, to contribute to discovering a solution to the outstanding questions of our day' (GS 10).Three related documents, approved before GS, have been grouped with it in the present book.

One is the *Decree on the Mass Media* (IM), since modern means of communication are one of the most characteristic influences on people's lives in the twentieth century. Another is the *Declaration on Religious Freedom*, whose opening sentence announces that 'the dignity of the human person is a concern of which people of our time are becoming increasingly more aware' (DH 1). A third

LIVING IN THE MODERN WORLD

Pastoral Constitution on the Church in the World of Today (GS)

Related documents:

Decree on the Mass Media (IM)

Declaration on Religious Freedom (DH)

Declaration on the Church's Relation to non-Christian Religions (NA)

document is the *Declaration on the Relationship of the Church to non-Christian Religions* (NA), which introduces its subject with the phrase 'in our age, when the human race is being daily brought closer together'. This third group of documents opens up a number of typically modern questions which are not easily resolved, but which invite Christians to continuing study and reflection.

FOCUS ON EDUCATION

Underlying the entire experience of the Council is the realisation that continuing education can help us as the People of God to make sense of our lives and play an active, responsible role as members of our Church.

Vatican II's *Declaration on Christian Education* (GE) refers mainly to young people in Catholic schools, but a major concern of the Council and of *Living and Sharing Our Faith*, a National Project of Catechesis and Religious Education (of which this present book forms a part) is the education of the adult Catholic community. This very book originated from a desire to make a contribution to this vital task.

That is why our fourth and final focus will include examples of the burning importance of adult education in the thought and writings of the Second Vatican Council. This is not only frequently implied in the documents but it is often called for explicitly, as when SC 19 asks for people to be given a liturgical formation so as 'to foster their taking an active part in the liturgy, both inwardly and outwardly, in ways suited to their age, the circumstances they are in, the kind of life they lead, and their level of religious culture'.

In memorable words, GS 31 declares: 'We may rightly judge that the future of humanity is in the hands of those who can hand on to posterity grounds for living and for hope'. Unless they have reasons for living and hoping, people become disillusioned with life and overwhelmed with its pressures.

Where do we find the answer to the questions of life? In the words of Vatican II's last document, 'It is for God's people as a whole, with the help of the Holy Spirit, and especially for pastors and theologians, to listen to the various voices of our day, discerning them and interpreting them, and to evaluate them in the light of the divine word, so that revealed truth can be increasingly appropriated, better understood and more suitably expressed' (GS 44).

EDUCATING THE PEOPLE OF GOD

Declaration on Christian Education (GE)

Examples are given of the explicit and implicit call, throughout the Council documents for an educated adult Church.

NOTE

The previous pages (19-21) have offered an overview of the Council's achievement. Readers will find a fuller picture in the sixteen summaries of the documents contained in Part Two.

These summaries do not claim to be an adequate substitute for a detailed examination of the documents themselves, but will help readers to appreciate the scope and importance of the Council.

The Impact of the Council

Thirty years on, where has the Council taken the Church? And where is it still leading the Church? We have chosen three ways to answer these questions:

- by asking Catholic parishioners;
- by highlighting the key teachings of the Council;
- by examining the Council's underlying assumptions about the Church.

THE PEOPLE'S VIEW

Reactions to the Council have varied enormously over the years. For instance, here are some reactions from parishioners of Bushey parish in Hertfordshire. People were asked to describe how they experienced the Church before the Council and how they experienced it after the Council.

Before the Council

- The Church lived in a cut and dried way, where everything was black and white. God was stern.
- At its best, the Church was a safe rock that never changed. This was seen above all in the Mass, which was always celebrated in the same mysterious way.
- At its worst, the Church engendered fear about sin and anxiety over confession.

After the Council

- The Church is more welcoming and people share more. God is a friend.
- At its best, people are more involved and feel freedom of spirit. This is seen in the new form of celebration of Mass.
- At its worst, the Church is too flexible and confused. Some people drift away because of too much change; others because of too little.

Do you identify with these or similar experiences?

You may like to reflect on this and discuss it with somebody else. You may wish to disagree with them, if, for instance, you feel that they caricature the beliefs and practices of a previous generation. Don't be afraid to share your views.

At a conference in May 1994, a group of adult Catholic teachers from various dioceses of England and Wales were invited to think about Vatican II, thirty years after it had happened, in relation to the Church and world of the 1990s. The group used some of the material from this book. Here is a random selection of some of the hopes and dreams for their lives and work which people expressed. You may like to return to this list, agreeing and disagreeing with some of the points raised, and adding your own comments.

To promote places of truly free dialogue, as a preamble to structural change.

Vatican II is a pearl of great price. It is an iceberg, only one eighth of which is visible.

I want a Church which takes education seriously in all areas.

I realise that I am living out Vatican II when I ask 'What is a human being?'

There is a spirituality in the life of every person. The poorest and non-believing students enrich a school. I hope to embrace this insight.

The Church of Vatican II is well placed to contribute to the current educational debate about the spiritual and moral development of young people.

Vatican II has been with us for thirty years. The wine must have matured by now, and it's time we opened the bottle. The laity is the sleeping giant.

As a school governor, I shall try to promote evangelisation, an open admissions policy and spending which reflects the theology of Vatican II.

I experience some sadness about certain realities coming from the Vatican today, which contrast with some values associated with Vatican II.

I want to learn to stop and revisit brokenness.

The seeds of the word have been planted in sacred places.

moral choice

Thinking with the Church was never an easy option: 'Will you also go away?' John. 6) was the question put to those who experienced hard sayings from the Lord. It is no surprise, therefore, that the Council itself poses a moral dilemma.

Some people received the new vision with joy and excitement, and then inevitably experienced disappointment in the daily reality of Church life. Others were not able to receive new teaching or insights enthusiastically, however, and hesitated to accept change. So for both a disappointed enthusiast and for a cautious hesitator, the decision to stay with the Church remains a profound moral choice.

AN ABC OF THE COUNCIL

The Council's own view of the task facing the Church is expressed in a memorable sentence already quoted: 'The future of humanity lies in the hands of those who can hand on to posterity grounds for living and for hope' (GS 31).

The Council provided a series of pointers as to how the Church can fulfil this task. Some of these are new insights, others are neglected insights from the past. Let's call them *An ABC of the Council*.

ACCEPT

The Council invites Catholics to accept certain features of the Church's life:

- Accept that the Church is a sacrament of Christ offering life to the world.
- Accept the Word of God by reading scripture, by celebrating the liturgy and by being aware of the work of the Spirit in experience. In this way, the life of the Church is rooted in God.
- Accept that all members of the people of God, lay people and priests, have an apostolate to carry out. In this way, the Church is fully alive and all fulfil their vocation.
- Accept the local leadership of your bishop and the universal leadership of the college of bishops as well as the leadership of the Pope. This builds up both the local Church and the universal Church. In this way, the Church will grow in that unity of love which is a mark of the Church.
- Accept the variety of local Churches by encouraging each to express the Gospel in ways appropriate to their local culture. In this way, the Church is seen to be truly universal.

BEWARE

The Council invites people to be aware of certain modern threats to peace and justice:

- Weapons of mass destruction must never be used and disarmament must be pursued urgently;
- Anti-semitism must be opposed vigorously and the people of Israel respected as God's first chosen people;
- Lack of religious freedom must be opposed so that the Gospel may be freely preached everywhere and embraced freely by all who wish.

CHANGE

The Council invites all Catholics to make change part of their Christian life. This may mean:

- Responding creatively to the signs of the times;
- Admitting their need to turn away from sin and be renewed, because there is always need for reform;
- Understanding the new sciences so that Christian morality and doctrine can work in harmony with them;
- Creative involvement in the evangelisation of culture through the possibilities offered by the mass media.

DIALOGUE

The Council invites Catholics to be open to dialogue with all people of good will.

- Dialogue with Christians is to be pursued in discussion and in prayer together.
- There is value in dialogue with all those who believe in God and with all those who seek him.
- The world of today needs to hear the Gospel and the Church needs to hear the insights of the world. This is a vital part of the evangelisation of the world today.

EVOLVE

Under the guidance of the Holy Spirit, certain aspects of the Church's life will evolve to meet the needs of the world of today:

- A renewed liturgy will help people to celebrate the paschal mystery with greater participation and understanding.
- The ministries of bishop, priest and deacon will develop in accordance with the Church's renewed understanding of itself.
- Lay people will be invited to play a more active role in the life and mission of the Church.

Drawing all this together, it is as if the Council is saying:

People of God,

ACCEPT **the presence of the Lord in your midst, and**

BEWARE **of certain threats to full human life;**

Welcome *CHANGE* **and enter into**

DIALOGUE **with others, so that the life of the Church**

may *EVOLVE* **to meet the needs of the world of today.**

dream a dream

Christians everywhere will work for peace and justice.

All religious communities will renew themselves with sensitivity in accordance with the founder's charism and the signs of the times.

Education in the Church will evolve to offer formation to Christians at every stage of their life.

make an ABC

As you read about the documents in Part Two, you might like to recall this ABC and add to the authors' ideas, or subtract from them.

In the course of your own study of the documents you may wish - as an individual student or working as a group - to create an alphabet of your own as an aid to remembering the messages of Vatican II.

UNDERLYING ASSUMPTIONS

As well as its explicit teachings, the Council makes some underlying assumptions. We present four of these, each relating to one of the four focuses through which we have presented the Council documents.

THE FOCUS ON SPIRITUALITY

• *The Council assumes that people can come to know God through human experience as well as Revelation.* This is reflected, for example, in DV's teaching that the purpose of God choosing the people of Israel 'was that Israel might learn by experience how God acts towards human beings'. This new emphasis has encouraged ordinary people and clergy to see God at work in their daily lives. Spirituality is being attentive to the God who speaks not only in Word and Sacrament but also in daily life as many saints have shown.

THE FOCUS ON THE CHURCH

• *The Council assumes that the Church is multicultural and international.* For the first time ever the Church met as a truly multicultural and international body. Karl Rahner, one of the great theologians of Vatican II, went so far as to say that for the Church, the Council was 'the first act in history where the world Church first began to exist as such'. This has given heart to the Churches of the developing world.

THE FOCUS ON THE CHURCH IN THE WORLD

• *GS assumes that the world is the place of our salvation.* The Bible has two meanings of 'world': one describes the area of sin in our lives : 'Do not love the world or the things in the world' (1 John 2:15); the other emphasises God's love: 'God so loved the world, that he gave his only Son' (John 3:16). The second meaning is particularly strong in GS.

THE FOCUS ON EDUCATION

• *The Council assumes that the People of God will learn new ways of living out the faith today.* Almost every document assumes a continuous process of growing and learning.

This is a fitting note on which to end Part One. We have traced the main threads of the Church's life from its first encounters with the modern world through to its teaching in the Council about how to respond to this new situation. We have pulled together these threads by examining the impact of the Council. Finally, we offer a process for working with the Council documents (p 27).

A Process

In the first part of this book we have reflected on experiences of the Church before Vatican II, before looking at the main teaching and significance of the Council. In the second part we will approach each document using a similar process. We will look at the lived experience of the past, reflect on what the Council actually said, observe the strengths and limitations of each document, and consider how it has influenced the Church in the years since the Council. You may enjoy doing something like this to deepen your awareness of where we are and how we live in the Church today. We offer a model showing how this might be applied to the *Decree on the Apostolate of the Laity (AA)*.

STEP ONE: TO SEE WHERE WE CAME FROM

Can you, or any of your fellow parishioners, recall the old days before Vatican II?
What was it like to be a Catholic and member of a parish?
Do you agree with the comments of the Bushey parishioners (see p. 23) or with information offered about the background of AA? (see p.58-59)

STEP TWO: TO UNDERSTAND THE DOCUMENT

What did AA say about the place of lay people in the Church?
What changes were introduced as a result?

STEP THREE: TO SHARE INSIGHTS AND RESPONSES

What do you find helpful to your understanding of your place as a Christian? Have you any problems with them?

STEP FOUR: DISCUSS A POSSIBLE WAY FORWARD – WHERE DO WE GO FROM HERE?

Think again about what changes have taken place since Vatican II. Discuss which of these benefit us most as Christians. (It may be helpful to look at other documents and build up awareness of how the Council was answering similar questions in these. LG, the basic document for AA, may be useful).

STEP FIVE: MAKE A PRACTICAL PROPOSAL OR PLAN FOR THE FUTURE

i. for each person in their own life as a Christian;
ii. for the group or the parish.

This process offers a way towards a clearer perception of what it is to be a Christian today, and towards ways in which we could provide coming generations with 'reasons for living and hoping' (GS31).

In choosing to use this process, any group of the people of God may work together, moving confidently to discern how the Holy Spirit is calling and guiding the Church in our time.

Parishioners at Bushey where the work on this book began

Part Two: Towards an Understanding of Vatican II

*The whole Church carries forward the insights of a Council
and works out their implications*

Part Two invites you to look more closely at each document. The treatment of each offers:

an **introduction**
background
a **summary of content**,
strengths
limitations.
developments (*What came next?*)

At the end of each document, there are **discussion suggestions** and **questions** to help you to evaluate the insights of Vatican II in the light of what you have read, as well as in the light of your own experience.

As you examine these documents, you might consider whether you would draw up a different list of threads and assumptions from those suggested by the authors.

When you have read the summary of each Council document, you are invited to read the Vatican II document for yourself and make your own summary; or perhaps, if you are working in a group, appoint a willing member of your group to do it.

How does your summary compare with that of the authors of this book? What essential points would you wish to emphasise?

Focus on Spirituality

Vatican II's first document the Constitution on the Sacred Liturgy (Sacrosanctum Concilium) presents the Church's understanding of its worship and life of prayer.

Later, in the Dogmatic Constitution on Divine Revelation (Dei Verbum) the Council offers a deeper reflection on the relationship of God with believers.

Constitution on the Sacred Liturgy

(*Sacrosanctum Concilium* – SC)

what is liturgy?

Liturgy is the official public worship of the Church.

what is the paschal mystery?

This is the whole action of Christ saving humanity from sin, by offering himself as a sacrifice. The liturgy celebrates this sacrifice by re-enacting the life, death and resurrection of Christ. By this re-enactment, we enter more deeply into the Mystery of Christ's sacrifice and the work of our redemption is achieved.

Restoring the celebration of the Paschal Mystery to the centre of the liturgy has been one of the main achievements of liturgical reform.

INTRODUCTION

According to SC 10, 'The liturgy is the high point towards which the activity of the Church is directed and, simultaneously, the source from which all its power flows out'. The basic text of SC was written during two years of preparation for the Council. It draws on the immense amount of study, thought and pastoral experimentation developed by leaders of the twentieth-century liturgical movement. (See Background section below.)

SC is widely recognised as Vatican II's first major achievement. In introducing many changes into the way Catholics worship, SC, and the many documents which followed it during the years after the Council, showed very obviously that to live was to change.

BACKGROUND

Liturgy has been changing ever since the early Church began to move away from its Jewish origins, so renewal has been characteristic of liturgy from the beginning. The Council's renewal builds on a liturgical renewal movement that had been gathering momentum within the Church during the previous 100 years.

The 16th Century

In 1570, acting on the advice of the Council of Trent, Pius V published a detailed Order of Mass in Latin to be followed by virtually all Catholics. Prior to this, several dioceses had their own rite of Mass, but, in view of Protestant reforms, it was now felt necessary for all to follow the same rite. Every word and gesture was regulated, while the voice of the people remained silent as it had done for centuries. This 'Tridentine Mass' in Latin continued almost entirely unchanged for 400 years.

At that time, the Church was gathering her strength to fight off the attack of the Reformation. The sense of siege brought about an exaggerated idea of unity as uniformity and this was reflected in the liturgy. As time went on, some of these unifying elements lost their meaning; Latin, for example, was understood by fewer people.

Restoration and Discovery

During the 19th century, historians realised that since the Middle Ages the people had become more remote from the liturgy, both physically and psychologically. They came to 'hear' mass but followed their own devotions; the liturgical action was followed when a bell summoned the people's attention, as they had no words or role in the rite.

Led by Dom Prosper Guéranger (1805-1875), some French monks set about restoring the central place of liturgy. By rediscovering the original forms of ancient rituals and music, they hoped to make the liturgy both more intelligible and more beautiful.

The 20th Century

At first, this movement was largely confined to monasteries. A more widespread phase began under Pope Pius X. Communion had been an infrequent event and was first received aged 12–14 after Confirmation. In 1910 Pius X encouraged frequent communion and lowered the age of first communion to 7– 8 years old. People increasingly used missals (mass books) to follow the action. These reforms were introduced to help the people participate but the liturgy itself remained unchanged.

The work of the movement continued and received formal encouragement from Pope Pius XII in 1947. He emphasised that liturgy is not just carrying out ceremonies correctly; it is the prayer of Christ in which all should participate.

During the 1950s, the Holy Week services were restored to their ancient pattern. The development of the 'dialogue mass' brought the voice of the people into the liturgy in saying or singing Latin responses, though the response was hesitant. There was discussion about using the people's language but little progress.

In general, overt participation in the liturgy itself (as opposed to personal devotions) was weak; reform of the liturgy itself was minimal. Yet all the background work by scholars and imaginative pastors proved to be the vital backdrop to the Council's renewal of the liturgy.

what is a sacrifice?

'*A sacrifice is whatever work is accomplished with the object of establishing our holy union with God*'. (St. Augustine)

It means literally 'to make holy'; so to offer a religious sacrifice is to make something holy by offering it to God. Jesus offered all his work to God the Father. When he was told to stop his work of healing and preaching, he refused. His refusal led to his execution. So then he offered his own death to the Father, the ultimate sacrifice. Because he was 'one with the Father', Jesus rose from the dead. In his Spirit, he now offers to the Father the actions of all his followers and makes good our failings.

Summary

But the hour is coming, and is now here, when the true worshippers will worship the Father in spirit and truth..

John 4:23

The Introduction

The first sentence of SC was the first statement of the Council to the world. The Council announced its intention:

- 'to improve the standard of daily Christian living among Catholics;
- to adapt those structures which are subject to change so as better to meet the needs of our time;
- to encourage whatever can contribute to the union of all who believe in Christ;
- to strengthen whatever serves to call all people into the embrace of the Church'.

The renewal of the liturgy is seen as especially important in enabling the Church to carry out these intentions, since it is the liturgy which builds up the Church of Christ.

Chapter 1: (paras 5 - 46) **General principles regarding the renewal of liturgy**

In the liturgy certain changes are based on the nature of the liturgy, which is the worship of the community, led by the bishop, through signs accessible to the senses, by which Christ is made present to his Church (7); Before people can come to the liturgy, they must be called to faith and conversion (9).

Fostering liturgical formation and active participation:

The Church... wants all believers to be led to take a full, conscious and active part in liturgical celebration (14). This involves special formation for the clergy as well as for the people.

The renewal of the liturgy:

Parts of the liturgy subject to change may need to be reformed by those with authority; The importance of Scripture in the liturgy is emphasised (24).

Certain norms for change derive from the hierarchy and belong to the community; other reasons for renewal stem from the educational and pastoral nature of the liturgy: for instance, rites should be simple and intelligible – there may be scope for using the local language.

The liturgy may need to be adapted to different temperaments and traditions, in ways approved by local church authorities. The encouragement of liturgical life in the diocese and the parish depends on bishops, parish priests and on 'a flourishing sense of community' in a parish (42).

Liturgical commissions are needed, with experts who have various skills, to promote pastoral liturgy.

Chapter 2: **the holy mystery which is the Eucharist** (paras 47-58)

The Church does not want believers to attend the Eucharist 'as if they were outsiders or silent onlookers' (48); the structure of the Mass needs to be made more simple, 'so that it becomes easier for the people to take a proper and active part' (50).

The Bible is to be opened more widely to provide a richer diet of God's word (51).

The 'prayer of the faithful' is to be restored (53).

'There may well be a suitable place for the local language' to be used, as well as Latin (54).

People are encouraged to receive holy communion, sometimes under both kinds.

Priests are invited to concelebrate at certain masses.

Chapter 3: **the other Sacraments, and sacramentals** (paras 59-82)

These help to sanctify practically everything which happens in life, so 'it is most important that the people can easily understand' their symbolism (59); they may be celebrated in the local language according to revised rites.

The catechumenate for adults is to be renewed. (64)

SC adds, though not in much detail, that individual sacraments and ceremonies are to be revised.

Chapter 4: **the Divine Office** (paras 83-101)

The Roman Office corresponds to the rhythms of the day. It is to be modified 'in such a way that all to whom it is handed on will be able to enjoy it more easily and more fully' (90). Various details about the content and recitation of the Office are provided.

Chapter 5: **the liturgical year** (paras 102-111)

The Church unfolds the whole mystery of Christ over the cycle of the year, from his incarnation and birth to his return to heaven, to the day of Pentecost, and to our waiting for our hope of bliss and the return of the Lord (102); as well as celebrating the feasts of saints.

Sunday is the fundamental feast day (106).

Then Jesus said, 'I am the bread of life. Whoever comes to me will never be hungry, and whoever believes in me will never be thirsty.

John 6: 35

The liturgical year, its seasons and feasts, are to be revised, with special importance being attached to Lent and Holy Week.

Chapter 6: the music of worship (paras 112-121)

The musical tradition of the Church 'constitutes a priceless treasure' (112):

Gregorian chant occupies a 'special' place (116);

'religious singing by the people is to be encouraged' (118);

new settings of musical texts for the liturgy are to be developed.

Chapter 7: the art and furnishings of worship (paras 122-130)

The Church has always been a friend of the fine arts (122).

Worship provides scope for contemporary art, from every part of the world.

I am the living bread that came down from heaven. Whoever eats of this bread will live forever; and the bread that I will give for the life of the world is my flesh.

John 6:51

STRENGTHS

This was the first Council to think out the liturgy from basic principles. It made available the best of Christian liturgy from earliest times and presented this in a contemporary way. This reflected Vatican II's desire to be truly pastoral by feeding people's faith.

• A fundamental gain is awareness of the important roles of both laity and clergy in the liturgy. The whole assembly of God's people is now the subject of the liturgical action, not just the priest. *what is the participation*

This theological perspective has all kinds of practical consequences. Among these is the use of the local language to enable everyone to carry out their role more intelligibly and more fully.

• Liturgy is given a central place in the life of the Church as a community, not just in the individual's private spiritual life. Sacraments are seen as communal rites in which the community responds to God's initiative.

• The theology of the Word is renewed by restoring the liturgy of the Word in its own rite, in the Eucharist and in other celebrations. 'Christ himself is speaking when scripture is read in church'. (7).

• The theology of the Eucharist is developed. It moves towards a more deeply biblical understanding of sacrifice as self-giving exemplified by the love of Christ.

• An important distinction is acknowledged. 'The liturgy consists both of a part that cannot be changed, insofar as it has been divinely laid down, and also of parts which in the course of time can vary'. (21). The changeable elements will be developed for educational purposes and for adaptation to different temperaments and traditions of peoples. *what are they?*

• The development and reform of the sacramental rites is directed to a wider interpretation of sacrament beyond the concept of a single spiritual moment. A sacrament is seen as a celebration of the truth already lived out by the Christian. The celebration in turn enables people to carry on Christ's action more effectively in their lives.

LIMITATIONS

For all its undoubted strengths, this Constitution is not without its limitations.

Theology

• The work of our redemption is seen as a central feature of the liturgy but SC might be accused of too narrowly identifying this with liturgy. In a secular age, the church needs to show more clearly the connection between life and liturgy; the work of redemption is achieved in both contexts.

• Later Council documents represented a development in the Church's understanding of itself: in particular LG's emphasis on the priesthood of all believers, and the further development of this in GS's profound linking of faith and life. Such developments were unable to affect SC which had already been promulgated.

Practice

• The lack of liturgical understanding and readiness for change among ordinary clergy and faithful was far greater than the Council realised. An enthusiasm for change was not enough; time and effort were, and are, needed to carry through this far-reaching reform.

• Catholic liturgy has been stripped of its more obscure features; this is meant to set people free to celebrate and to highlight the fundamental mystery of the continued presence of Christ. Sometimes, however, the only change has been the stripping away, with no use made of the new freedom; this leaves colourless and lifeless liturgy. Alternatively, it led to an aggressive attempt to force participation on uncomprehending and bewildered congregations. The stripping away has also led to some architectural insensitivity in redesigning churches for the new liturgy.

• Ultimately, the celebration of the new liturgy is dependent on the growth of real communities to celebrate it. The building up of community life is a fruit of the liturgy but communities must first want to be built up.

WHAT CAME NEXT?

Vitality and Pluralism

The new rites led to a flourishing of creativity in a wide variety of ways ranging from music and texts to movement and decoration. This meant liturgy no longer only expressed unity by uniformity but also by local diversity. This diversity was expressed by local adaptations of the Roman rites (SC 37-40) under the jurisdiction of local bishops. (LG 26).

Promoting Change

The publication of the new liturgical texts took some twenty years to complete, beginning with the new Roman Missal in 1969, including the Rite of Christian Initiation of Adults (RCIA) in 1974, and the revised Order of Christian Funerals in 1985.

As well as the books themselves, there were numerous instructions on how to use the books in line with the intentions of the Council. This has proved the biggest difficulty, with great variations between countries. Some countries have liturgical centres and formation teams (as suggested in SC); others do not.

While the first versions of all the books and texts are now in place, there is still work to be done. Continual revision is part of the work of implementing the liturgical spirit promoted by the Council. For example, the revision of the Roman Missal is currently (in 1994) in its final stages. The willingness of local bishops to adapt the liturgy for their culture and the availability of resources for this also varies greatly.

Opposition to Change

Change can often be painful: the difficulty was to communicate the meaning and purpose of the change. It soon became clear that liturgical renewal involved more than a series of adjustments to age-old ceremonies.

People's responses varied from enthusiasm to rejection. Some people liked the quiet murmuring of strange and mystical sounds (the sacred Latin language) in a contemplative atmosphere, which suggested the awesome 'otherness' of worship, and they disliked the invitation to participate more overtly. They also regarded the use of Latin as a symbol of unity and catholicity.

questions on the document

1. Why did the Council wish to renew the liturgy?

2. Eucharistic Prayer 3 (Roman Missal) was composed after Vatican II. You are invited to read this and examine its principle themes in relation to the Council's emphases. What do you discover?

3. Discuss the different considerations which need to be remembered if liturgy is being planned to become more alive and real in our lives.

If you are working in a group, take time:

TO SEE where we came from

TO UNDERSTAND the Constitution

TO SHARE insights and responses

DISCUSS a possible way forward: where might we go from here?

MAKE a practical proposal or plan for the future.

Although it was not the intention of the Council to abolish them, Latin and the Gregorian chant are now used infrequently; some people see this as the betrayal of a whole sacred tradition. For them the loss of the Tridentine Mass was a bereavement from which their faith has hardly recovered. Archbishop Marcel Lefebvre was able to build on this sense of loss and finally led a small group out of communion with Rome under the banner of the 'old ways'. (In reality, however, the position of Lefebvre was as much to do with objections to the whole Council agenda as it was to do with liturgy.)

Participation

The greater participation of the people was the yardstick which the Council gave itself for judging the success of its liturgical reforms. While there is increased vocal and musical participation, perhaps the greatest challenge has been to enable people to participate with their whole life.

This is seen vividly in some of the simple celebrations among Catholics in the less developed countries who have grasped the spirit of the liturgical reform with remarkable speed; their lives often revolve around liturgy as their one celebration of hope.

In many places, however, the gap between liturgy and life is still considerable. This gap is heightened by a lack of agreement in some places on how much the clergy should dominate the planning and celebration of liturgy, and on how much they ought to involve parishioners in expressing their insights and experiences.

Sacraments other than the Eucharist

The new rites of baptism, marriage, penance and anointing of the sick have been generally well received. They combine the timeless prayers of tradition with the personal experiences of the participants. Revision and improvement continue.

This happy blend of the old and the new expresses a sense of the present moment standing between the past and the future. In this way, these sacraments show that Christian faith is a way of life, a way of being in the world rather than a way out of it.

Constitution on Divine Revelation (*Dei Verbum* – DV)

INTRODUCTION

[handwritten: Very important document! (Answers the question 'How can we know God?)]

It is easy to see why Cardinal Suenens referred to DV as 'the jewel of the Council'. The original draft was rejected after an emotive debate in 1962 and it took four years for the final version of this short document to be approved. As he introduced the final version, Archbishop Florit observed that the history of DV 'has fused with the history of the Council into a kind of unity'. DV expresses some of the most significant shifts in theology which occurred during the Council. It set some fundamental areas of Catholic theology in a new and positive context, which underlies much of the reform in other documents of Vatican II.

BACKGROUND

The Bible is central to Christian faith of any kind, yet the reading of the Bible by Catholics in their own language was restricted between 1564 to 1897. Why?

The ban in the sixteenth century was imposed to stop the spread of Protestant Bible translations. The Catholic Church insisted that the Bible should not be available on its own but should always be accompanied by official, traditional interpretation. Protestant theology insisted 'scripture alone' was needed, while Catholic theology insisted on 'scripture *and* tradition'. Lying behind this is one of the central questions of religion, the question of revelation: how can we know God?

One Catholic answer was: through accepting the doctrines of the Catholic Church. The Church possesses God's revelation in the deposit of faith, a set of propositions drawn from scripture and tradition; God can be known from nature, but can only be fully known by accepting these supernatural truths. In 1870, Vatican I had reaffirmed this propositional view of revelation. The twentieth century saw developments in two vital areas concerning revelation: the nature of revelation itself and attitudes to the Bible.

Revelation

Firstly, the nature of revelation was seen to be broader than a set of propositions. In the 1950s, Karl Rahner was teaching

divine revelation

God reveals himself to us in different ways.

This Word of God, God speaking to humanity, is the message of salvation for all people.

that God reveals *himself* rather than ideas about himself. At the same time Bernard Lonergan was exploring human experience rather than the mind as the place where God does this revealing. There also arose a new kind of biblical theology that took the Bible on its own terms rather than as a sourcebook for texts to prove Catholic doctrine; tradition added nothing to the once for all revelation found in scripture. These views were all suspect before the Council and in our description of the strengths of DV we will show how the Council brought them together at the heart of the Church's renewed understanding of revelation.

Biblical Criticism

Secondly, attitudes to the Bible had changed. Until the nineteenth century, most Christians assumed that the words of the Bible should be taken literally. During the nineteenth century there grew up among some Protestants a liberal school of biblical criticism, based on new archaeological evidence and new theories about how the bible was written. In its extreme form, it denied any historical value to the gospels, seeing them as pure myth. Such liberal theories shocked Catholics and so fears of liberalism and protestantism came to dominate Catholic attitudes to Bible study.

With Pope Leo XIII, however, there emerged the beginnings of the Biblical Movement. This had two dimensions: the encouragement of bible reading and the application of critical historical methods to interpretation of scripture. In 1890, the Ecole Biblique was founded in Jerusalem, the first Catholic institute for the study of the Bible. In 1893, the Pope tentatively encouraged the study of the Bible in the light of new discoveries. In 1897, Catholics were given permission to read approved translations. Following the condemnation of Modernism, Catholic scholars again became cautious, but in 1943 Pope Pius XII gave formal approval to modern methods of study and encouraged Catholics to read the Bible.

The climax of the biblical movement came in 1956 when the Ecole Biblique published the Jerusalem Bible (English Edition 1964) with explanatory notes that recognised the presence of different literary styles. Even so, some Catholic scholars remained under a cloud. But the growth of Catholic Bible study groups, and the availability of a critical edition of the Bible approved by the Church marked a definitive break with past attitudes.

Chapter 1: Revelation in itself

God in infinite love speaks to humankind as friends and enters into their life, so as to invite and receive them into relationship with himself. The pattern of this self-revelation of God unfolds through deeds and words (2) .

In this way, down the centuries, God prepared the way for the gospel (3).

In response to God's revelation, our duty is the obedience of faith, a total and free self-commitment to God (5).

Chapter 2: The transmission of divine revelation

Christ our Lord, in whom the whole revelation of God is summed up, entrusted the apostles with his gospel. The apostles left as their successors the bishops (7). Thus the apostolic preaching, which is expressed in a special way in the inspired books, was to be preserved by a continuous succession until the end of time. There is growth in understanding of what is handed on, both the words and the realities they signify (8).

Hence sacred tradition and scripture are bound together in a close and reciprocal relationship (9).

The task of authentically interpreting the word of God has been entrusted only to those charged with the Church's ongoing teaching function. This teaching function is not above the word of God but stands at its service (10).

Chapter 3: The divine inspiration of holy scripture and its interpretation

In the process of composition of the sacred books God chose and employed human agents, using their own powers and faculties, in such a way that they wrote as authors in the true sense; we must acknowledge that the books of scripture teach firmly, faithfully and without error such truth as God, for the sake of our salvation, wished the biblical books to contain (11).

If interpreters of holy scripture are to understand what God wished to communicate to us, they must carefully investigate what meaning the biblical writers actually had in mind. In order to get at what the biblical writers intended, attention should be paid to literary genres (12).

God has made known to us the mystery of his will, according to his good pleasure that he set forth in Christ, as a plan for the fullness of time, to gather up all things in him, things in heaven and things on earth.

Ephesians 1: 9

Chapter 4: The Old Testament

God intended the salvation of the entire human race. In preparation for this, he chose a people for himself. His purpose was that Israel might learn through experience how God acts towards human beings. This plan is there in the books of the Old Testament (14). The plan and pattern of the Old Testament was directed above all towards the coming of Christ (15).

Chapter 5: The New Testament

The Word of God shows its force supremely in the New Testament (17).

The four gospels are historical documents. First, the apostles passed on to their hearers what Jesus had said and done. Next, inspired writers composed the four gospels. They selected some things from the abundant material already handed down, orally or in writing. Other things they synthesised, or explained with a view to the needs of the Churches (19).

Chapter 6: Holy Scripture in the Life of the Church

The Church has always held the divine scriptures in reverence no less than it accords to the Lord's body itself. (21).

The Church strives to attain an ever deeper understanding of holy scripture. The Council encourages those members of the Church who are engaged in biblical studies. (24). Biblical translations should be published, equipped with explanatory notes, so that members of the Church can become familiar with holy scripture and can become soaked in its spirit (25).

The words that I have spoken to you are spirit and they are life.
John 6:63

STRENGTHS

• The whole tone of this constitution marks a major shift in Catholic attitudes. Revelation is presented not as the passing on of information but as personal encounter. 'It is precisely this personal element that is brought into the foreground in this constitution: God does not simply increase men's store of speculative knowledge; he addresses them as his friends.' (C. Butler *The Theology of Vatican II*, DLT, 1981)

Revelation proceeds from the person of God and reaches the personal centre of human beings, not just their minds. The original acts of revelation are the creation and the history of Israel, the life of Christ and the early Church; all these are people's encounters with God described in the Bible. The fact that this revelation is complete does not stop the event of revelation from continuing.

As we read the Bible and listen to it in liturgy, we are led to encounter God more fully in scripture, in life and in prayer. Using the image of the Church as the bride of Christ, DV affirms that 'the God who spoke of old still maintains an uninterrupted conversation with the bride of his beloved Son' (8).

• This 'uninterrupted conversation' leads the community of believers to formulate doctrines which express new understandings of God's revelation. In this way doctrine will always be developing in order to re-express the original encounters of revelation for new generations and cultures.

The Council affirms this development of Christian doctrine: 'Growth in understanding comes about through contemplation and study by believers; through the intimate understanding of spiritual things which they experience; and through the preaching of those who, on succeeding to the office of bishop, receive the sure charism of truth'. (8). So development derives from the living experience of believers as well as from the Church's teaching authority. This affirmation of development and experience as elements of tradition overcame the fear that all such talk was Modernism. It led to a flourishing of modern Catholic theology.

• This attitude to development explains the Church's approach to scripture and tradition as part of one event, Revelation. 'Tradition and scripture together form a single sacred deposit of the word of God' (10).

Scripture does not need tradition to make up for a lack of some elements of revelation. Tradition is the explanation of scripture handed down through the centuries. 'Catholics do not say that scripture is defective, but that tradition is needed for a discovery of the full contents and implications of scripture'. (Butler, *ibid*)

As an example of this, we would cite the doctrine of the Trinity. This doctrine is rooted in the sayings of Jesus and the writings of Paul but its clear statement as three persons in one God is found in later tradition. This presentation of tradition and scripture as a unity was a vital emphasis for enabling dialogue with Protestants.

• This personal and dynamic view of revelation is greatly assisted by the application of critical historical methods to the interpretation of the Bible. Such methods often show the hidden depths of texts and help believers to contemplate them more profoundly.

The Constitution steers between the extremes of either taking every word of the Bible literally or rejecting every word as untrue. The key to this is to understand the intentions of the Biblical writers: 'truth is expressed differently in historical, prophetic or poetic texts, or in other styles of speech' (12).

The Constitution accepts that the Gospels are a unique blend of history and theological interpretation: the apostles passed on their stories after Jesus' resurrection not in a straight narrative but 'with the fuller insight which they now possessed', an insight 'learned by experiencing the glorious events of Christ and by enlightenment from the Holy Spirit' (18). In this way, the Council has enabled the Church to adopt a balanced, modern approach to the study of the Bible.

• The insistence that 'ignorance of the scriptures is ignorance of Christ' (St. Jerome quoted in DV 25) shows the seriousness with which the Council wants Catholics to approach the Bible. It really is for all, and the prayerful reading of it should underpin all the Church's activity, so that 'spiritual life will receive a new impulse from increased devotion to the Word of God' (26).

LIMITATIONS

DV is weakest in its discussion of the Old Testament. There is a tendency to see it wholly as preparation for Christ rather than having value in itself. Since the Council, the combined effect of more Biblical studies and better relations with Jews has led to a fuller appreciation of the value of God's self-revelation in the Old Testament.

Not enough credit to Jewish understanding

By shifting the emphasis from propositional to personal revelation, DV inevitably raises questions of authority. The Church does still subscribe to propositions in creeds, for example, even though it now sees these elements of tradition in a new light. There can be tension between believers who claim a personal understanding of revelation that differs from the orthodox tradition. This has always been the case, but DV has encouraged all believers to reflect on revelation in their lives and so tension is more likely than before.

The Constitution resolves this tension by stating that the authentic interpretation of revelation is the task of the 'magisterium', translated here as 'the church's ongoing teaching function'. This function is usually exercised by bishops.

DV presents this as part of a trio: 'tradition, scripture and the church's teaching function are so connected and associated that one does not exist without the others, but all together contribute to the salvation of souls'. (10). The relationship of these three is described in other Council documents on the Church and on bishops. There continue to be tensions, however, over the authority and extent of the Church's teaching function.

WHAT CAME NEXT?

• The work of the Biblical movement ceased to be the work of a minority of scholars and became the concern of many Catholics. In Catholic schools and parishes the prayerful reading and the study of scripture are now integral parts of formation in faith. In universities, Catholic scholars can now contribute to the scientific study of the Bible. Fathers Raymond Brown, Joseph Fitzmyer and Roland Murphy, editors of *The New Jerome Biblical Commentary* (1968) are examples of scholars who have helped Catholics not only to come to terms with biblical criticism but also to see it as an enrichment of faith. In 1964, just before DV was approved

questions on the document

1. In what events and situations of your life has God been revealed to you?

2. How do you see the importance of both doctrine and scripture in understanding and meeting God?

3. What are your favourite passages from the Old Testament and the New Testament? Why?

If working in a group, explain your choice to other members of the group.

If you are working in a group, take time:

TO SEE where we came from

TO UNDERSTAND the Constitution

TO SHARE insights and responses

DISCUSS a possible way forward: where might we go from here?

MAKE a practical proposal or plan for the future.

by the Council, the Pontifical Biblical Commission published a document affirming in greater detail some of the methods of biblical criticism referred to in DV. Biblical criticism is now regarded as the ally rather than the enemy of Catholic faith.

• The reading of the Bible privately or in groups has now become common among Catholics. Many Catholics now meet in groups to share prayer and reflection centred around the Bible. They meet to listen to the Word of God and concentrate on the interplay between the word and life. Sometimes these groups develop so strongly that they become small communities. In Latin America, there has been a growth of 'basic Christian communities', where people share the word and share their lives. Such groups are also particularly fruitful settings for Catholics to meet with other Christians.

• The reform of the liturgy undertaken by the Council presupposes DV's approach to revelation. Readings from scripture in the language of the congregation are now central to liturgy; preaching is usually a homily relating them to the life of the hearers. This has been a dramatic change away from silent readings of the Latin text, followed by a course of sermons instructing people in the truths of the faith, without any reference to the scriptures.

• The whole style of Catholic theology has become profoundly biblical. For example, the Council's own decree on priestly formation emphasises that 'the study of scripture ought to be the soul of all theology'. The shift in emphasis from propositional to personal revelation is also reflected in theology. In his encyclicals, Pope John Paul II repeatedly quotes from GS 22: 'It is Christ who fully reveals humankind to itself' (*Redeemer of Humanity*, 8; *Rich in Mercy*, 1).

Focus on the Church

For Catholics the Church is central to our understanding of life. The Dogmatic Constitution on the Church (Lumen Gentium) presents the fullest, most detailed understanding of the Church ever developed by a Council.

The practical application of this theology is offered in five Decrees which consider different groups within the people of God. These are:

Decree on the Apostolate of the Laity (Apostolicam actuositatem)

Decree on the Pastoral Office of Bishops in the Church (Christus dominus)

Decree on the Ministry and Life of Priests (Presbyterorum ordinis)

Decree on Priestly Formation (Optatam totius)

Decree on the Sensitive Renewal of Religious Life (Perfecta caritatis)

Three other Decrees also reflect the Church's understanding of itself:

Decree on the Eastern Catholic Churches (Orientalium ecclesiarum)

Decree on Ecumenism (Unitatis redintegratio)

Decree on the Missionary Activity of the Church (Ad gentes)

Constitution on the Church (*Lumen Gentium* – LG)

INTRODUCTION

In many ways, this Constitution is the central document of the Second Vatican Council. It offers a rich theology of the Church's inner life, and it has been very influential since the Council. The final document is the third draft of the Constitution, and it reflects dramatic changes in the thinking of the Council fathers. More time was allocated to its discussion than to any other topic. Its scope and depth developed considerably before the final text was approved during the third session of the Council.

Many other Council documents depend on LG, especially those grouped together with it in this section. As will be seen, these expand the implications of the theology of LG, applying it to various groups within the Church.

BACKGROUND

Definitions of the Church at the start of this century concentrated on the Church as a perfect society, the only institution with religious truth in a world of falsehood. Heretical views were excluded by means of rules laid down by authority. During the first half of the century, however, two developments began to move the Church beyond this view.

For practical reasons, the institutional authority of the Church needs the active rather than the passive cooperation of the laity. In the 1920s Pius XI encouraged the collection of Catholic Associations known as Catholic Action. Lay people worked with the clergy to promote Christian living in a variety of ways; for example, Catholic professional guilds, Catholic scouts and guides, young Christian workers. This was described by the Pope as 'participation by the laity in the apostolate of the hierarchy'. It was not yet seen as people exercising their own apostolate of the laity.

In theology, the Christian theologians of the first centuries, 'the Fathers', were being studied afresh. They too lived at a time when the Church was struggling to establish itself in a hostile world. From them emerged the richly biblical theology of the Church as the mystical body of Christ, as the place where people come to know Christ personally and where Christ gives life to the world. This theology went well with the practical developments in Catholic Action and it was given formal approval by Pius XII in 1943 with his encyclical letter 'On the Mystical Body' (*Mystici Corporis*).

The Second World War was a watershed in the development of the Church's self-understanding. France was declared to be a mission country needing new Church methods to reconvert it. Germany had to find new ways to rebuild a shattered society and a shattered Church. Initiatives came by looking in two directions at once, back to the sources (or Christian origins) and ahead to the modern world.

Fathers Marie-Dominique Chenu, Yves Congar and Henri de Lubac were three French theologians who examined key areas in this way. They discussed the relation of grace to nature, the role of the laity, Christian unity, adaptation of Church structures. They expressed their explorations in the language of the Bible and the Fathers, a language very different from the medieval, scholastic theology of Church teaching at that time. This new style led to problems and all three were suspended from teaching or writing for brief periods. Yet they were to exercise a vital influence on the Council and de Lubac was finally made a Cardinal.

Summary 9

1. The Mystery of the Church

The Church is in Christ a sacrament or instrumental sign of union with God and of unity with all humanity (1).

The Church owes its existence to Jesus Christ, sent by the Father to be the Redeemer, and to the Holy Spirit, sent to sanctify the Church on the day of Pentecost. He leads it into all truth and he makes it one in fellowship and ministry (4).

A variety of biblical images describe the Church (5-7). It is a visible structure, a community of faith, hope and love, which subsists in the Catholic Church, although many elements of sanctification and of truth are found outside this (8).

In St Augustine's words, the Church 'proceeds on its pilgrim way amidst the persecutions of the world and the consolations of God'.

2. The People of God

God sanctifies people by setting them up as a people who serve him in holiness. Christ is the head of this people: his Church is the new Israel, which never ceases from renewing itself (9).

All God's people share in the one priesthood of Christ, made holy by the sacraments, sharing Christ's prophetic role and graced by the gifts of the Spirit (12).

 This pilgrim 'Catholic Church' is necessary for salvation. Catechumens belong to it (14).

 The Church is joined to other baptised Christians who do not profess the whole faith, with whom it seeks unity (15).

Those who have not yet accepted the Gospel are related to the people of God in various ways: Jews, Muslims and all who search for God are specified. By preaching the Gospel, the Church draws its hearers to faith, so that they build up the body of Christ (17).

3. The Hierarchical Constitution of the Church

The Lord instituted a variety of ministries which are directed towards the good of the whole body (18).

St. Peter and the apostles constitute one Apostolic College: so in a similar way the Roman Pontiff and the bishops are joined together. The supreme power over the whole Church

And I, when I am lifted up from the earth, will draw all people to myself.

John 12:32

which this College enjoys is solemnly exercised in an Ecumenical Council (22). The role and infallibility of the Pope as defined at Vatican I is reaffirmed (25).

Bishops lead 'local churches', gathered around the Eucharist, governing them as Vicars of Christ, not as vicars of the Pope (27).

Bishops exercise their ministry with priests and deacons. The diaconate is to be restored as a ministry in the Church, even for some living in the married state (29).

4. The Laity

The laity are all Christ's faithful, incorporated into Christ by baptism and sharing Christ's priestly, prophetic and royal office. Their special vocation is to seek the kingdom of God by engaging in temporal affairs and ordering these in accordance with the will of God (31).

The apostolate of the laity is a sharing in the Church's mission of salvation (33).

Lay Christians are dedicated to Christ and anointed by the Holy Spirit. They are called to be heralds of faith - through them the Church can become the salt of the earth. Pastors are to promote the dignity and responsibility of the laity in the Church. Every individual lay person ought to be a witness to the world of the resurrection and life of the Lord Jesus and a sign of the living God (38).

Do you not know that you are God's temple and that God's Spirit dwells in you.

                    1 Corinthians 3:16

5. The Universal Call to Holiness in the Church

Everyone in the Church is called to holiness (39), to the fullness of the Christian life - which is conducive to a more human way of living (40) in faith, hope and love. This applies to priests, lay people in various states of life and to all who are crushed by hardship. True disciples of Christ are characterised by love for God and for their neighbour.

6. Religious

Some priests and some lay faithful are called to religious life, consecrated to God in chastity, poverty and obedience. Their spiritual life must be dedicated to the good of the whole Church (44).

Religious should try hard to ensure that through them the Church more effectively shows forth the real Christ to believers and unbelievers (46).

7. The Eschatalogical Character of the Pilgrim Church and its Union with the Heavenly Church

The pilgrim Church on earth awaits Christ's coming in glory (49), joined in communion with the saints in heaven, imitating their example and helped by their intercession.

8. The Blessed Virgin Mary

The Church venerates the memory of the blessed virgin Mary, mother of God, its model in faith and love (53).

The Son of God took his human nature from his mother, whose role is described in the New Testament. We have one Mediator, Christ (60), but, since Mary cooperated in the work of the Saviour, she is invoked by the titles of advocate, benefactress, helper and mediatrix. She is the type of the Church, a model of holiness and Christian life, and, as such, is venerated by Catholics. She shines forth as a sign of sure hope and comfort for the pilgrim people of God (68).

We know that all things work together for good for those who love God, who are called according to his purpose.

Romans 8:28

52

STRENGTHS

This Constitution is the first time the Church has ever portrayed herself at length. The Council examined the Church's internal relations in this Constitution and its external relations in the *Pastoral Constitution on the Church in the World of Today.*

Cardinal Suenens invited the Council to answer the question: 'Church of Christ, what have you to say about yourself?' LG answers this question in a tone that leaves behind the anti-protestant and anti-modernist style that had dominated official teaching. Instead, the text is woven from the Bible, the Fathers and human experience.

The Church is a Christ-centred mystery

The Church here moves away from seeing itself primarily as a religious organisation concerned with right order. It is a community formed by Father, Son and Holy Spirit, raised up in history as a sign of God's Kingdom and best defined in dramatic, biblical images.

The Church of Christ is also defined in a way which does not confine it within the limits of the Roman Catholic Church which is its fullest manifestation. Other Churches participate in the reality of the Church as mystery in varying degrees.

The Church is the whole People of God

The Church emphasises here that it is made up of all its members, not just priests and religious. This people is on a pilgrimage, a journey; and human beings can make mistakes and will be constantly developing. Nevertheless, this community is the necessary way to salvation because Christ is the way and Christ is present to us in his body, the Church.

The Church now recognises that Christians not in full communion with the Pope are nevertheless joined to the Catholic Church in other ways. It also recognises that it is joined to others who believe in God or who seek him with a sincere heart. This emphasis on unity with all Christians and all humanity is a crucial development.

The Church is led by the bishops

The Council stresses that the function of all authority is service, not domination. The Church has two levels of authority, the local Church and the universal Church. Each local Church has its bishop as its sacramentally ordained leader. All the bishops together constitute a college with the Pope as its head. This collegiality shows that the Church is truly 'catholic' (universal). The College and the head share the task of leadership and the gift of infallibility which the Lord promised to the Church. This restores the balance left incomplete by Vatican I. (see pp. 10-11)

Bishops ? infallible

Lay people are called to share in the mission of Christ

By baptism, lay people are given a role in the mission of Christ; so it is their own apostolate and is not given to them by the clergy. This is a liberating insight for all lay people but also a responsibility.

The Church is called to be holy

The Church, the people of God, is holy because it is the body of Christ, endowed with the gift of the Holy Spirit, which means it is called to be fully human and to live in love, strengthened by Scripture and prayer. So not only is the Church holy by definition but everyone in the Church is actually called to become a holy person. *Duh?*

The Religious Life is a gift to the Church

Following on from the above, the religious life is seen not as individual perfection but as a special way of belonging to the Church, a way that can show Christ powerfully to the Church and the world.

The Church has no abiding city here on earth

This means that the Church no longer claims to be simply identical with all that is meant by the Kingdom of God; it is poised between the now and the not yet. United to the saints in heaven, the pilgrim Church on earth is provisional rather than triumphalist.

Mary is the model of the Church

The Council decided not to publish a separate document on Mary, but wisely, from an ecumenical point of view, linked her to the Church. Mary is a model of the Church because both are the place where Christ comes to birth in the world. The Council affirms that the cult of Mary enriches Christian life but needs to be promoted in ways that avoid credulity and promote true faith in Christ.

LIMITATIONS

• The issue of the role of women in the Church is not addressed. The fact that the Church is now able to address this issue is a fruit of the new openness created by the Council, but the absence of any specific discussion in LG is striking. The issue was already there in society, as is seen from a reference to it in the *Church in the World of Today* (GS), but the Council did not realise the need to address the question of how this affected the Church.

• The renewed understanding of the Church as the whole people of God has opened up rather than resolved two complex issues: the role of authority in the Church and the role of priests.

• LG represents a great advance away from the negative tone of anti-protestant and anti-modernist arguments that often characterised Catholic statements about the Church, towards a positive tone and a biblical style. Yet compared with its counterpart on the *Church in the World of Today* , LG has a more assertive tone and does not share that document's sense of searching. It is a Dogmatic Constitution which draws on a long tradition of theology of the nature of the Church. It also needs to be interpreted in the light of the *Decree on Ecumenism* (UR).

WHAT CAME NEXT?

This was only the third document approved by the Council. It is the foundation text upon which the others build; in a sense, the whole Council is what came next. In the light of the theology of LG, all the Church's ministries and states of life needed redefining, as well as its relationship to other churches and religions; so the impact of the separate documents on those topics will be examined later. Two features of the Church as a whole will be examined now: firstly, the official meetings of national and continental groups of Churches held to apply Vatican II to their local situation; secondly, the movements which sprang up to enable clergy and laity to participate more fully as partners in the life of the Church.

Local Situations

Many bishops began to apply the Council's teaching on the local Church. For instance, at Medellin, Colombia, in 1968 and at Puebla, Mexico, in 1979, the bishops of Latin America made a sustained effort to work out together the

questions on the document

1. The Council uses these phrases to describe the Church: 'people of God'; 'pilgrim people'; priestly people'; 'called to holiness'; 'the mystery of the Church'. Choose two which you regard as especially important and explain why you choose them.

2. 'Vatican II says as much about the local Church as about the universal Church.' Do you agree? Discuss the implications of this.

3. What is the implication of presenting the Church as a 'pilgrim Church'? In this respect, how do you see the life of the Church developing in the future?

If you are working in a group, take time:

TO SEE where we came from

TO UNDERSTAND the Constitution

TO SHARE insights and responses

DISCUSS a possible way forward: where might we go from here?

MAKE a practical proposal or plan for the future

implications of the Council for their local Churches; the policies that emerged from these conferences shaped the life of these Churches in very distinctive ways. In England and Wales, a National Pastoral Congress was held at Liverpool in 1980 for bishops, clergy, religious and laity together to shape a response to the Council and to examine the English and Welsh Church in the light of Vatican II.

New Movements

New movements arose that fostered a greater sharing of life and prayer in the Church, often at the expense of the older forms of lay associations. There were new lay communities associated with religious orders, Marriage Encounter, the Neo-Catechumenate, Focolare and many more. One movement which affected many members of the Church after Vatican II was the Charismatic Renewal Movement and we will examine this more closely.

The roots of this movement do not lie explicitly in the Council, but without the Council the movement would not have grown in the Catholic Church. LG emphasised the Spirit dwelling in the hearts of all the faithful: the Spirit 'leads the Church into all truth, and he makes it one in fellowship and ministry, instructing it through a diversity of gifts both hierarchical and charismatic' (LG 4).

The charismatic gifts of prophecy, healing, speaking in tongues and others, were found in the early Church but sprang to life again in the Catholic Church, beginning in the USA, in 1967. Laity, clergy and religious met in prayer groups for informal prayer and for teaching, especially on the power of the Spirit. This spread rapidly round the world, supported by Cardinal Suenens who saw in it the spiritual dimension needed to carry forward the renewal begun by the Council. The movement received the approval of bishops and of Pope Paul VI.

From the perspective of Vatican II, the movement was important not so much for its emphasis on spectacular gifts but because it promoted among Catholic clergy and laity the active development of three of the four principal Constitutions of the Council. Firstly, the Bible is widely used in the movement. Secondly, the movement places great emphasis on rediscovering the power of the sacraments. This point combined with the first to produce an upsurge of liturgical music that was scriptural and singable in a very lively style of celebration. Thirdly, the movement gave many lay people their first experience of ministry and leadership, exercising the gifts or leading others in prayer. The movement affected all the Churches and many prayer groups are ecumenical, meeting another of the Council's aims.

The Constitution which the movement was accused of neglecting was GS. This led to conflict between those who emphasised social action and those who emphasised charismatic gifts. The movement is now less visible than in the 70s but many of its insights have been absorbed into the main stream of Church life.

In the consideration of the documents which follow, developments in the wider fields of parish and lay ministry will be developed in greater detail.

Decree on the Apostolate of the Laity

(*Apostolicam actuositatem* – AA)

INTRODUCTION

Most baptised Christian believers are lay people. It is an injustice to describe lay people negatively, simply as those who are not clerics. AG expresses it very succinctly when it says, 'The laity are those of Christ's faithful who have been incorporated into him by baptism and who live 'in the world' (AG 15).

When Newman was asked by a cleric 'Who are the laity?' he is said to have replied that the Church would look foolish without them. A common saying before Vatican II was that the duties of lay Catholics were to 'pray, pay and obey'. One of the Council's great achievements was to open up a theological and practical understanding of lay people in the Church. If the first question of the Council was 'What is the Church?', it was felt that the role of ordinary members of the Church needed to be reassessed.

The Church had never adequately discussed the way its ordinary members carry out their role of spreading the Gospel. The Council's decision to emphasise the people of God and the universal call to holiness laid the groundwork for this decree in providing its basic theology. As members of the people of God, lay people in the Church are called to Christian life and to witness to the resurrection in the world. While other documents (GS, UR, AG, GE) examine the world in which people live as the arena of the lay apostolate, this decree takes a more detailed look at lay Catholics and their mission.

BACKGROUND

Since the Middle Ages, there had been a tendency to identify the Church with the clergy. Lay Catholics tended to be ignored in official teaching, where it was usual to think of lay people as 'secular' (for example, in contrast with members of religious orders). Lay people were sometimes regarded as second class citizens in the Church.

The waning of the Church's political power in the 19th century helped to bring about a change: lay Catholics came to be seen as a force which could represent the Church in secular society. A revival of the 'body of Christ' theology emphasised the importance of each member, and helped set the agenda for the Council. (See background to LG, pp. 48-49).

Partnership between clergy and lay people grew as the Church became involved in mass education. Catholics were encouraged to band together in specialist work areas and in the professions for mutual support and 'Catholic action'. In the 20th century, new movements like the Young Christian Workers and the Legion of Mary grew up beside the older confraternities. However, all this 'lay' involvement was strictly controlled. There was little confidence shown by Church leaders in people's ability to care for the Church and its traditions. Fear was expressed that lay organisations might become political. Moreover the temper of the time often encouraged the hierarchy to take a paternalistic approach that was common throughout society.

As the 20th century developed, this was starting to change. Education and technology revolutionised society; colonialism declined, democracy became common. In all walks of life it became clear that people get involved in movements for social change when their role is not seen as secondary or derivative.

Another urgent pastoral reason for change sprang from the expansion of the Church and the shortage of priests. The involvement of lay people was urgently needed in the day-to-day mission of the Church in many parts of the world. There was a need to engender a sense of co-responsibility between lay people and clergy.

During the 20th century, certain Popes and theologians (like Yves Congar OP) had examined the theological basis of the role of lay people, so that, in a sense, Vatican II was catching up with what was already happening. Nevertheless, when AA was written there were no official precedents to follow, and the completed text was eagerly awaited.

family apostolate

AA 11 and 12 identify various aspects of family apostolate:

- *adoption of abandoned children;*

- *welcoming of strangers;*

- *help in managing schools;*

- *advice and help for adolescents;*

- *help in preparation for marriage;*

- *support for married people in material and moral dangers;*

- *provision for the elderly, not only for necessities but for a fair share in economic development.*

- *The energy of young people is to be appreciated, so that they can become apostles to their contemporaries and play their part in social and cultural life.*

Summary

Like good stewards of the manifold grace of God, serve one another with whatever gift each of you has received.

1 Peter 4:10

AA begins with a reference to the indispensable part played by lay people in the mission of the early Church, and notes that the modern world needs zealous lay Catholics. The decree makes clear the proper character of the lay apostolate, so that this can be incorporated into the reform of canon law.

Chapter 1: the vocation of lay people to the apostolate

The apostolate of lay people comes from the call of Christ. Scripture shows that 'lay people, sharing in the priestly, prophetic and kingly offices of Christ' play their part in the mission of the Church in the world (2).

There is one apostolate for the Church, but there are many ways of sharing in it. United with Christ, all members share his mission in the world, contemplating Christ in everyone, whether known to them or strangers. Some ministries are appointed by the Church while others are received through a special gift or inspiration of the Holy Spirit, not necessarily a spectactular gift, when people act with faith and generosity.

The work of lay people in the Church is incorporated into Christ's mission of love through the sacraments of baptism and confirmation, which create 'a royal priesthood and a holy people'.

Lay people must take care to develop their spiritual lives, supported by one another. Without this, mere activism is of no value.

Spirituality for lay people needs to be adapted to age, life-style and gifts, if it is to enrich Christian living. Mary's faith, hope and love provide a model of life in union with Christ.

Chapter 2: the aims of the apostolate

The mission of lay Christians is to renew the world of today by penetrating it with the spirit of Christ. Lay people join with clergy in this ministry of word and sacrament. They have a particular mission to look for opportunities to speak about Christ, and to bring Christ's moral principles to bear on the problems of the age. 'Let your light so shine before people that they may see your good works and give glory to your Father who is in heaven' (Matthew 5, 16). Lay Christians renew life in the world ('the temporal order') by promoting justice and renewing every sphere of society and culture.

Works of charity are at the core of the Christian message. Awareness of the world as one family has grown. Christians are called to reach out to those in need, in a spirit of service, with respect for the dignity of each one created in God's likeness. AA asks Christians to take account of the freedom and dignity of the person receiving help, with the greatest possible sensitivity and unselfishness (8).

Chapter 3: various fields of the apostolate

Important fields of work include church communities, the family, young people, society, national and international organisations.

Given that women's role is changing in society, women have a vital role to play in the apostolate. All share in Christ's mission in Church and world, as did the men and women who assisted St. Paul in preaching the Gospel.

The parish offers obvious scope for community apostolate, as does the diocese and wider fields. Christians gradually penetrate their living and working environment (13). People should minister to one another. For instance, the apostolate of married people includes their witness to the indissolubility of marriage, the education of their children, and their defence of the dignity and legitimate freedom of the family. There is also scope for the apostolate nationally and internationally.

Chapter 4: various forms of the apostolate

All action starts with the individual person's apostolate, which can be carried out anywhere, even in places where the freedom of the Church is curtailed. Associations may be helpful, inside and outside the Church. The way a person lives is a revelation of Christ, as well as the words that a person speaks. 'Let all call to mind that by public worship and prayer, by penance and the free acceptance of the toils and hardships of life which brings a likeness of Christ in his sufferings, they will reach out to all humanity and contribute to the salvation of the world' (16).

Where Catholics are few and scattered, they should come together in smaller groups as a witness of Christian love and for mutual support. Joint apostolates are appropriate in many situations; people can be apostles in their family and community, in their parish and diocese; or they can join associations. Working with others strengthens the sense of

...lead a life worthy of the calling to which you have been called with all humility and gentleness, with patience, bearing with one another in love, making every effort to maintain the unity of the Spirit in the bond of peace. There is one body, one Spirit, just as you were all called to the one hope of your calling...

Ephesians 4:3

common direction in spreading the Gospel and evangelising society, local and international.

'Catholic action' deserves special mention, but no one form of the apostolate is better than any other. Mutual cooperation is needed. Clergy should welcome and support the involvement of individual married or celibate lay people and special groups.

Chapter 5: preserving due order

Bishops are responsible for promoting and organising the lay apostolate, and priests may be able to offer special help. Catholics are urged to work alongside other Christians and those who respect Christian values, in mutual co-operation.

Chapter 6: formation for the apostolate

The apostolate requires appropriate education and formation, which has its own spirituality. Many skills are needed, both theoretical and practical. These need to be constantly studied and revised in the light of experience. Young people need special care and encouragement.
For everyone, formation for the apostolate is lifelong (29).

AA ends by calling each lay person to answer the call of Christ and become his co-operators in the modern world.

Keep alert, stand firm in your faith, be courageous, be strong. Let all that you do be done in love.
1 Corinthians 16:13

STRENGTHS

For some people, the greatest source of surprise was that such a decree should exist at all. It was, in a sense, a revolutionary document. Lay Catholics were coming of age in the Church. AA is a charter to which lay Catholics could appeal for inspiration and to know what is expected of them. The proper field of apostolate for lay people is at the centre of what the Church is about: 'to renew all things in Christ' (7). LG's fifth chapter on the universal call to holiness in the Church stresses 'the fruits of grace which the Spirit produces in all the faithful'.

LIMITATIONS

Although the Council gave great freedom and dignity to the apostolate of the laity, AA was not without limitations – it was of its time. For instance, the Council gave approval to organisations that see themselves as 'collaborating in the apostolate of the hierarchy' (20). This is inconsistent with a view of lay people as having a distinctive role in Christianising the world. Although AA recognised that a 'fuller' role should be found for women in the apostolate, since then, issues of justice have highlighted the problematic situation of women in society and in the Church. This has repercussions for the lay apostolate.

WHAT CAME NEXT

Many people were impatient about delays in implementing the Decree. Some parts of the Church found it difficult to move towards what some considered to be a revolutionary situation, though lay people are now usually encouraged to be actively involved in the Church's apostolate and to see themselves as being at the centre of the Church's mission to the world. Pastoral councils in dioceses, deaneries and parishes have helped to renew the structures and mission of the local Church. An increasing number of lay people have been trained as catechists and religious educators for dioceses and parishes. Lay Catholics are now involved in many aspects of ministry.

England and Wales

In England and Wales, 1980 saw the National Pastoral Congress in Liverpool, with representation from the whole Church: bishops, clergy, religious and lay people from every

from
the easter people

In the Congress in Liverpool the maturity, strength and apostolic courage of the lay delegates were clearly to be recognised, together with their desire for a more responsible role in the future. We should like to see the lay members of our Church, men and women, young and old, become steadily more aware of their true dignity in the people of God and of their daily calling as baptised Christians to evangelise the society in which they live and work.

Their role brings out an essential dimension of the work of the Church, an extension of Christ's kingdom to wherever they are in God's creation. For they are not simply delegates of the bishops and clergy, they are gospel-inspired lay people, members of the laos *(people) of God, and in their own right missionaries of Christ to the world* (27).

questions on the document

1. 'Mere activism is of no value' is a reflection on the temptation to 'do' rather than to 'be'. How might you reconcile the need to get things done with the importance of reflecting and praying?

2. Why did the Council stress the apostolate of the laity? How has this developed since Vatican II? How do you see it developing in the future?

3. Why are many young people 'put off' the Church? How can older Christians help them?

If you are working in a group, take time:

TO SEE where we came from

TO UNDERSTAND the Decree

TO SHARE insights and responses

DISCUSS a possible way forward: where might we go from here?

MAKE a practical proposal or plan for the future.

diocese. *The Easter People*, the Bishops' message at the end of the Council presented a vision to challenge the Church in England and Wales. The Congress had a major effect on the Church's sense of vocation and mission by emphasising that it was both necessary and praiseworthy for Catholics to consider the relevance of the Gospel in the world of today. There was widespread consultation to prepare for the exchange of views, and delegates were fully involved in the thought-process of the Congress. Initiatives to translate the impetus of the Congress into daily life were encouraged in several dioceses.

Synod Document

Following the 1987 Synod of Bishops, Pope John Paul II's letter on *The Vocation and Mission of the Lay Faithful in the Church and the World* (Christifideles Laici) developed the conciliar teaching of AA and emphasised that the formation of lay people is increasingly seen as a priority for the Church.

An important contribution of lay people has been in the ministry of justice and peace. There is a new respect for the importance of the basic values needed for human society and for the Kingdom of God to flourish.

However, the gap between theory and practice in the life of the institutional Church is at times acute. AA's vision of the people of God, gifted by the Spirit through baptism and confirmation with ministries and gifts for the Church, cannot exist alongside an exclusively hierarchical view of the role of the clergy which still dominates some parishes.

The whole Church has to face up to the challenge of this new era in its history: much constructive work has still to be done. New and demanding questions about ministry are still being raised. Though some fear the 'creeping clericalisation' of involved lay Catholics, others are working hard to develop a practical sense of collaborative ministry in Church communities.

On-going Vision

The Council's vision of the lay apostolate, and the breath and scope it brings to the Church's life continue to develop. In the post-Conciliar writings of Pope John Paul II this vision has been developed in relation to the apostolate of the laity and the essential mission of Christ and the Church:

Christifideles laici, 1988:

The eyes of faith behold a wonderful scene: that of a countless number of lay people, both women and men, busy at work in their daily life and activity, oftentimes far from view and quite unacclaimed by the world, unknown to the world's great personages but nonetheless looked upon in love by the Father, untiring labourers who work in the Lord's vineyard. Confident and steadfast through the power of God's grace, these are the humble yet great builders of the Kingdom of God in history (17).

Redemptoris missio, 1990:

People today put more trust in witnesses than in teachers, in experience than in teaching, and in life and action than in theories. The witness of a Christian life is the first and irreplaceable form of mission: Christ, whose mission we continue, is the 'witness' par excellence (Rev 1:5; 3:14) and the model of all Christian witness...

A commitment to peace, justice, human rights and human promotion is also a witness to the Gospel when it is a sign of concern for persons and is directed towards integral human development (42).

Decree on the Pastoral Office of Bishops in the Church (CD)

who is a bishop?

A Bishop has charge of a diocese.

what does 'pastoral office' mean?

'Pastoral' refers to the way a bishop should carry out his role, following the gospel teaching, like a 'good shepherd' or pastor.

INTRODUCTION

Whatever the origins of bishops in the early Church (about which there is some disagreement among scholars), in modern times bishops are named by the Pope each to take care of and nurture a diocese (a particular Church) which is a local group of Catholics. The diocese is divided into a number of parishes.

Vatican II spent much of its time and theological energy clarifying the place of bishops in the Church. This decree was intended to work out practical consequences of the doctrinal understanding of the role of bishops (see LG). CD spells out the ways in which a bishop carries out his ministry in the Church.

BACKGROUND

Vatican I had concentrated on working out a theology of the Pope. Vatican II complemented the earlier Council by devoting considerable attention to bishops, especially by its theology of the Episcopal College. This represents a return to a more collegial or 'shared' direction of the Church, and was intended to promote, as a practical reality, a sense of the universal Church as the communion of all the local Churches.

bishops' conference of england and wales

If readers consult the national Catholic Directory (published each year in an updated version), they will find a presentation of the membership of the Bishops' Conference of England and Wales, its General Secretariat and Standing Committee, its five Departments (each listed with its various component committees), as well as a list of official consultative bodies and Conference agencies.

The Risen Lord sent the Holy Spirit to his apostles 'to build up the body of Christ' (1). The Pope, as the shepherd of all the faithful, supports the bishops who take the place of the apostles as pastors or shepherds. United as a college they take care of all parts of the Church; as individuals they are leaders of 'particular churches' or dioceses.

1. Relationship between bishops and the Universal Church (4-10)

By consecration bishops become members of the college of bishops, united with the Pope and exercising authority throughout the whole Church. They are called to show special care for parts of the world where the Church is experiencing difficulties (e.g. missionary countries or lands where there is a shortage of priests).

Although the Pope, with his Roman curia, exercises authority over the universal Church ('for the good of the churches'), bishops are in authority over the faithful in their dioceses. The Council recognises the value of the Roman curia but asks for it to be reorganised and made more internationally representative and more ready to listen to the views of lay people.

2. Bishops and particular Churches or dioceses (three sections 11-35)

The first section deals with diocesan bishops, shepherds over their dioceses, who 'feed their sheep in the name of the Lord by fulfilling their office of teaching, sanctifying and governing them' (11).

They proclaim the Gospel, build up faith and teach Christian doctrine 'in ways relevant to the needs of the time' (13).

They exercise truth and charity by evangelising society and by teaching the faith to different groups of believers. They take good care of catechists, clergy, religious and laity, for bishops are servants of the community, 'good shepherds... true fathers who manifest a spirit of love and care for all' (16).

They foster ecumenism and promote the lay apostolate, taking care of those with special pastoral needs.

Bishops are independent of civil authorities, are appointed by 'competent ecclesiastical authority' (20), and are invited to resign when age or 'some other serious reason' prevents them from doing their work.

As the Father has sent me, so I send you.

John 20:21

The second section deals with diocesan boundaries, which may need to be reconstructed. Dioceses should be neither too large nor too limited, and may need to be reorganised with the help of 'competent episcopal conferences' (24).

The third section considers those who co-operate with the diocesan bishop in his pastoral work, including coadjutor and auxiliary bishops; other senior co-operators (diocesan officials and pastoral councils); diocesan clergy, especially parish priests and curates; and members of religious orders, who co-operate with the local bishop.

The gifts he gave were that some would be apostles, some prophets, some evangelists, some pastors and teachers, to equip the saints for the work of ministry, for building up the body of Christ..
Ephesians 4: 11-12

3. The co-operation of bishops for the common good of a number of Churches (36-44)

Bishops often need to pool their resources and coordinate their plans, using synods and councils, and collaborating with other Bishops in local 'episcopal conferences': 'a kind of assembly in which the bishops of some nation or region discharge their pastoral office in collaboration, the better to promote the good which the Church offers to people' (38); each episcopal conference draws up its own statutes and determines its procedures.

The boundaries of ecclesiastical provinces and regions may need to be revised, while pastoral needs may mean that certain bishops exercise interdiocesan responsibilities (e.g. bishops responsible for the armed forces).

Further directories concerning 'the pastoral care of special groups of the faithful' will need to be drawn up after Vatican II (44).

STRENGTHS

The document clarifies the relationships between local bishops and the Pope. Lying behind this issue is a history of power struggles between local bishops and the Roman curia. The document puts in place a theology of collegiality vital for the Church's development. It emphasises that it is by drawing on the gifts of the whole community that bishops can be good pastoral leaders in the local Church.

LIMITATIONS

Collegial government of the universal Church has not been easy to work out in practical structures and procedures (see the later treatment of universal synods below). There is a degree of confusion to be resolved (at a later Council of the Church?) about the theological relationship between bishops and priests, and also about the authority of national episcopal conferences. The 'local Church' envisaged by CD would appear to be a much closer relationship between parishes than exists in some vast modern dioceses.

WHAT CAME NEXT?

An important observable consequence of the existence of CD was that individual bishops became less remote and more accessible to the faithful in their local churches. When they act collegially (for instance in national or regional episcopal conferences), bishops are heard to speak with a unified and more prophetic voice in society (e.g. in relation to justice and peace issues, economic policy and other moral issues). This has been true of bishops in Latin America, in the United States, in Europe and elsewhere.

A practical consequence of the theological progress associated with the theology of CD is to be seen in the Synod of the universal Church, a consultative body of bishops established by Paul VI after Vatican II, which meets in Rome every three years. Synods have discussed important topics such as justice in the world (1971), evangelisation (1974), catechetics (1977), an appraisal of Vatican II (1985), the vocation and mission of the lay faithful in the Church (1987), priestly life and formation (1990) and the consecrated life (1994).

An important development since Vatican II has been the formation of national Bishops' Conferences, to express the unity of local Catholic churches. Through these the bishops of particular countries are united in reflecting and deciding on pastoral matters of national concern.

questions on the document

1. Who is your bishop? When and where have you met him?

2. 'CD offers a picture of a collegial church.' You are invited to illustrate and discuss this statement.

3. Discuss the various ways in which your bishop's work might be helped:

a) by parishes as a whole, or by groups in parishes;

b) by individuals who take up some mission, task or responsibility.

If you are working in a group, take time:

TO SEE where we came from

TO UNDERSTAND the Decree

TO SHARE insights and responses

DISCUSS a possible way forward: where might we go from here?

MAKE a practical proposal or plan for the future.

Decrees on Priestly Formation & on Ministry and Life of Priests

(*Optatam totius* – OT and *Presbyterorum ordinis* – PO)

Priests are 'ordained' or formally commissioned by the Church for the ministry of word and sacrament. They work with the bishop by taking care of parishes and other communities.

INTRODUCTION

In any period of change in the Church, the attitude of priests is a vital element in carrying forward reform. 'The desired renewal of the whole Church depends to a large extent on a priestly ministry animated with the spirit of Christ'(OT). The renewed understanding of the Church set out in LG posed a challenge for priests. The Council became aware that the priest's role is one 'of daily increasing difficulty in the renewal of the Church' (PO). After some hesitation, caused by fears of overloading the agenda, the Council issued two documents: one about training, the other about priestly ministry and life. We will deal with them together.

BACKGROUND

For centuries, the clergy were seen as clearly separate from and even 'above' lay people in the life of the Church. It was accepted that there were two kinds of Christian: the clergy, celibate and apart, were assigned to the service of God and prayer; the laity, living in the world, came to church to receive God's grace and teaching passed on by the priest. This picture of priesthood had been severely strained during the Second World War which had shaken the fabric of society. In France, priests had secretly accompanied their parishioners to the prison camps by dressing in lay clothes and living with them in the camps. After the war, Church leaders saw that French society had become thoroughly secular. Cardinal Suhard, Archbishop of Paris, estimated that one million people in Paris had never had any contact with the Church, so he launched Mission de Paris; drawing on the experience of the prison camps, priests lived as workers. This experiment was fraught with difficulties yet it showed an awareness that new approaches to priesthood were needed. On the other hand, many bishops were ignorant of or disapproved of these experiments and wanted to affirm a modified version of the traditional model, drawing on the best of priestly practice current at that time. This tension is seen in PO.

After reminding the Church that everybody has the duty of fostering vocations to the priesthood, the document stresses the central role of seminaries in training priests. Those who teach in them should be chosen from among the best, while selection and assessment of students should be firm; even though there is a shortage of priests, standards should not be compromised.

Spiritual formation should be integrated with doctrinal and pastoral studies. Christ is the centre of the students' formation. They should seek him in prayer, in the bishop and in the people, 'especially the poor, little ones, the sick, sinners and people with no faith' (8). They should be so formed in celibacy that they receive it as a gift not as an imposition, while being made aware of the difficulties of chastity in present-day society (10).

Seminary training is to be carried out in accordance with modern insights about psychology and education. The discipline of the seminary should encourage increasing self-discipline as the student matures. Among the qualities to be fostered are sincerity, care for justice, faithfulness to promises, courtesy, modesty and charity in speech (11). Consideration should be given to raising the age of admission to the priesthood (12).

Studies in theology and philosophy should lead to greater understanding of human life and of the life of Christ. As well as the Christian tradition of philosophy, they should also study those new philosophies and advances in science which have a particular influence in their own country. ' The study of scripture ought to be the soul of all theology... Dogmatic theology should be so arranged that the biblical themes are first propounded' (16).

Then they should study the development of doctrine and how these truths can be communicated today. 'Special care is to be taken for the improvement of moral theology' (16).

Pastoral training is also needed. 'In general, those gifts are to be developed in the students which most favour dialogue with people. Such are the capacity of listening to others and of opening their hearts in a spirit of charity to the various circumstances of human need' (19).

Summary 9

Priestly Formation

But you are a chosen race, a royal priesthood, a holy nation. God's own people, in order that you may proclaim the mighty deeds of him who called you out of darkness into his marvellous light.

1 Peter 2:9

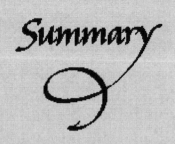

Summary 9

Ministry and Life of Priests

For as often as you eat this bread and drink the cup, you proclaim the Lord's death until he comes.

1 Corinthians 11:26

1. The priesthood in the mission of the Church

The priest is a collaborator with the bishop who shares in the bishop's mission and authority, a mission and an authority given by Christ. The chief responsibility of a bishop is the holiness of his priests.

2. The ministry of priests

For the priest, his first duty is 'to announce the gospel of God to all'. He does this in a variety of ways, preaching so as to 'apply the enduring truth of the gospel to the concrete situations of life' (4).

Through the celebration of the sacraments, especially the Mass, the priest leads people to union with God and gathers people into one fellowship; priestly authority is given for the sake of the body, the Church. 'Of little use are ceremonies, however beautiful, or societies, however flourishing, if they are not geared to producing Christian maturity'. While the priest should care especially for the vulnerable and the young, 'the task of the pastor is not limited to care of individuals, but extends to the formation of real Christian community' (6).

Relation to others: The bishop and his priests work as one and priests support each other, whether as teachers, as manual workers or as pastors. Priests are brothers to all the faithful and 'should confidently entrust responsibilities to the laity in the service of the Church, giving them scope and freedom for action, and indeed inviting them when appropriate to take up works on their own initiative' (9).

3. The life of priests

Call to perfection: The priest's spirituality should be rooted in the following of Christ by meditating on his life in scripture and by celebrating his presence in the sacraments. Through their prayer and ministry, and especially by harmonising these two aspects of their life, they grow in holiness.

Spiritual needs and aids to the life of priests: In order to carry out the divine work to which the Holy Spirit has called them, priests will show obedience to God by being responsive to the needs of the people and the leadership of the bishop. Through celibacy and simplicity of life they will be more fully conformed to the pattern of Christ. Priests will find nourishment from spiritual practices such as retreats. They will find support in having opportunities for study. They will benefit from vacations and from having adequate means by which to live.

STRENGTHS

The two documents depict the priesthood with a new breadth of vision. Priesthood is not just centred on liturgy and on church law. The formation, ministry and life of the priest are centred on the gospel and on the human person. The first duty of the priest is to proclaim the gospel. In order to do this, he must be attentive to the human culture of those to whom he is sent and attentive to his own need for personal support. The development of his own humanity is a key element of his priestly training and life. Here are some of the implications of this vision of priesthood.

• The training of priests emphasises that theological study should be centred round the great themes of the Bible. This is a move away from narrower theological systems.

• There is an emphasis on love and involvement. The priest is united in brotherly love with his fellow priests and his bishop. Similarly, he is involved in the life of the people.

• The priest leads a balanced life and seeks holiness by integrating his work and his prayer. The climax of this process is the celebration of the Eucharist.

• Without detracting from the gift of celibacy, the value of married priests is affirmed as part of the tradition of the Eastern Catholic Churches.

• By emphasising the priest as a minister of the Word as well as a minister of the Sacraments, the way is opened for dialogue with Protestant churches about priestly ministry.

• Priest workers receive a measure of approval: 'they share the lot of manual workers when this is approved as expedient by the relevant authority' (8). Some saw such approval as unfortunate but the French bishops pressed for it. It showed the Church is willing to approve pastoral initiatives in the area of ministry and priesthood.

1. Is there any aspect of the priesthood that you would want to see changed? If so, why and how?

2. What is 'collaborative ministry'? In what ways could collaborative ministry be developed in your local church?

3. What do you consider to be the strength of Vatican II's vision of the priesthood?

If you are working in a group, take time:

TO SEE where we came from

TO UNDERSTAND the Decrees

TO SHARE insights and responses

DISCUSS a possible way forward: where might we go from here?

MAKE a practical proposal or plan for the future.

LIMITATIONS

The documents about priests were both prepared somewhat hurriedly. PO appeared only when the bishops protested that they wished to have a full decree on the priesthood. The result is that there are limitations. We highlight three:

• There is a certain lack of dynamism, caused by an emphasis on the priest as deriving from the bishop. While strictly correct, it does not make for a strong affirmation of the priest.

• There is none of the sense of involvement in the world that characterises GS. In fact, GS and PO do not fit together easily. The question how far priests should be involved and how far separate from the world of lay people is one that causes much debate. The decree did not discuss it at any length.

• The often difficult experience of priests themselves seems lacking from the decree. The world is frequently indifferent to religion and can leave the priest feeling isolated. On the other hand, people ask priests many practical questions which they may feel unqualified to answer. Having raised the issue of priesthood, the Council did not bring it to a satisfactory conclusion.

WHAT CAME NEXT

In response to the new vision and the new sense of brotherhood, priests were encouraged to meet to reflect on their role. Programmes such as the Ministry to Priests offer personal support among priests. Meetings in deaneries offer support for pastoral work. In England and Wales, an experimental initiative was an elected assembly of priests called the National Conference of Priests. It first met in 1970 and then became established as an annual four day assembly which has met ever since. Similar assemblies now meet in most countries.

In England and Wales the National Conference of Priests was the seed-bed from which sprang the National Pastoral Congress in 1980. This Congress was a moment of joint reflection by laity and clergy on the role of the Church in Britain. Some were disappointed by its lack of radical proposals. Yet viewed in retrospect, some see this Congress as the Church in England and Wales passing from a childlike, passive conformity to a mature and adult

Christianity. The laity became confident that they could work as partners with the clergy, each respecting the other. This partnership was a major fruit of the new vision of priesthood.

Many priests now live out a ministry centred around life in their parish rather than around a clerical world apart. Priesthood is now shared, and exercised in different ways by the ordained minister and by the lay person. Collaborative ministry is not only a division of tasks between lay people and clergy but also a real sharing of responsibility for all dimensions of the Church's life.

The 1990 Synod of Bishops focussed on the theme of priestly formation, affirming and deepening the Council's teaching. The Synod Document *Pastores Dabo Vobis* presents a dynamic vision and speaks strongly about the partnership between priests and all the baptised.

Many would say, however, that, since the Council, there has been a growing crisis in the Catholic priesthood. Some priests have experienced a loss of identity; many have left the priesthood; the number of vocations has declined noticeably. The long tradition of priestly celibacy is seriously questioned.

Taken together, the sense of partnership and the sense of crisis are leading the Church to a deeper reflection on the nature of ministry and priesthood. The priesthood of all believers and the ministerial priesthood are both in a state of development.

Decree on the Sensitive Renewal of Religious Life

(*Perfectae caritatis* – PC)

What is meant by 'religious life'?

In religious life, some Christians publicly consecrate their lives to God, living in communities or as hermits.

All witness to, work for, and pray for the building up of God's Kingdom on earth.

INTRODUCTION

Although the 1929 code of Canon Law had tried to standardise the forms of religious life, several initiatives to reinvigorate them and make them more relevant to the modern world had been developed in Rome and elsewhere after the Second World War. These involved attempts to change outmoded customs, notably ones which affected women's orders. Vatican II set out to answer the question 'What sort of religious life is appropriate for today?'
A renewed theology of religious life was offered in chapter 6 of LG. This section was inserted after the Council's presentation of the universal call to holiness, in this way setting aside an earlier understanding of religious life as a 'state of perfection' superior to that of lay Catholics. The 25 articles of PC spell out the basic principles of renewal applicable to the many varieties of religious life in the Church.

BACKGROUND

Religious life developed in the Church from the 3rd century, under the influence of various founders, foundresses and reformers. This book does not offer details, but any Catholic encyclopedia offers information about the major developments and directions.

The modern renewal of religious life began during the pontificate of Pope Pius XII (1939-58), with various international commissions and encyclicals. The Roman Congregation for Religious set up a commission for reform in the 1940s. New types of 'secular institute' were recognised in 1947, and, around the time of Vatican II, books like Cardinal Suenens' *The Nun in the World* suggested ways in which traditional styles of apostolic religious life could be modernised.

The time was thus ripe for the more radical renewal introduced into religious orders, as into every part of the Church, by Vatican II.

1. The Gospel Counsels

The starting-point for PC is 'the practice of the gospel counsels, the search for true charity' based on the teaching and example of Jesus. Observing the counsels of chastity, poverty and obedience, religious dedicate themselves to the Lord, following Jesus closely and adding to the richness and creativity of the Church's life and mission (1).

The sensitive renewal of religious life involves a return to the sources of Christian life in general and to the original inspiration of forms of religious life, modified where necessary to suit new circumstances.

2. Five principles underlie this renewal:

a) religious life is essentially about following Jesus;
b) each form of religious life has its distinctive spirit and tradition which derives from its founder;
c) all religious foundations are to enter into the life of the broader Church and to promote the Church's initiatives;
d) current needs and insights are to be discerned enthusiastically for the sake of the mission;
e) spiritual renewal is a priority in renewing religious life.

3. Lifestyle

Religious communities are asked to adapt their style of life, prayer and work to suit modern needs and conditions. Every member of the religious body is to participate in the renewal. General Chapters of religious orders are the usual authority to oversee the adaptation.

Religious are reminded of the gospel virtues to which their dedication commits them. Seeking God before all things, nourished by Scripture and the Eucharist, they are called to develop a spirit of prayer and give themselves to the God of love.

4. Variety

PC points to the variety of forms of religious life: contemplative and monastic communities, lay and clerical apostolic institutes, congregations specialising in pastoral work, and secular institutes.

5. Commitment

The meaning of religious commitment to chaste celibacy, Christlike poverty and self-sacrificing obedience is explored in some detail (12-14).

If you wish to be perfect, go, sell your possessions, and give the money to the poor, and you will have treasure in heaven; then come, follow me.

Matthew 19:21

Truly I tell you, there is no one who has left house or brothers or sisters or mother or father or children or fields, for my sake and for the sake of the good news, who will not receive a hundredfold now in this age - houses, brothers and sisters, mothers and children, and fields, with persecutions - and in the age to come eternal life. But many who are first will be last, and the last will be first.

Mark 10:29-30

questions on the document

1. What do you think religious communities contribute to the life of the Church and the world?

2. Why and how has religious life changed since the Council?

3. Religious take three vows of celibacy, poverty, obedience: What is the meaning of these three vows today?

If you are working in a group, take time:

TO SEE where we came from

TO UNDERSTAND the Decree

TO SHARE insights and responses

DISCUSS a possible way forward: where might we go from here?

MAKE a practical proposal or plan for the future.

Models for community life and for apostolic zeal are offered by the New Testament. External expressions of religious commitment (like enclosure and religious dress) may need to be updated. Religious formation will play a key part in renewing religious life, as will the development of individual talents and skills and new apostolic methods.

The importance of promoting religious vocations among young people is recognised; and 'religious must recognise that the witness of their own way of life is the best recommendation of their own foundation' (24).

PC ends with an appreciative reference to 'the very profusion of the work, whether manifest or hidden, done by religious' (25).

STRENGTHS

In its own 'return to the sources', PC shows a movement away from the legalistic formulae in which religious life had been described. Its forms are essentially ways of following Christ, rooted in ancient tradition but adapted for the modern world. While religious are reminded of the gospel values on which their vowed life is based, they are given freedom to adapt their attitudes, structures and rule of life to new situations. Each religious family is offered the impetus to rediscover its founding inspiration and to adapt its life-style to suit its contemporary mission. While preserving its distinctive features, each institute is called to take part in the overall renewal of the whole Church. For individuals, the emphasis is on personal call and response, continuing formation, professional training, and on the essentially spiritual nature of religious vocation.

LIMITATIONS

Although PC recognises the distinctiveness of each religious family, these are still grouped together as variations of one basic model. While some institutes had hoped for a more complete and detailed document, the virtual absence of apostolic religious (especially religious women) from Vatican II made this hope unrealistic. Some religious feel that PC hardly does justice to the origins and mission of their community. Moreover, the powerful new impetus which Vatican II gave to the vocation and mission of lay people in the Church perhaps inevitably led to a decreasing appreciation of the value of religious life.

WHAT CAME NEXT?

The renewal inaugurated by Vatican II was necessary but often misunderstood. Sometimes enthusiasm for change led to abuses and a decline of fidelity. Failure to attract younger members has been seen as evidence of uncertainty, inadequate leadership, and lack of a clear vision, but the reasons are more complex. For instance, factors such as increasing secularisation in western society and the growth of lay apostolates help to explain this crisis. The usefulness of the mission of some institutes has been questioned. On the other hand, a greater sense of collaborative ministry has opened up religious institutes to sharing their mission and spirituality with lay colleagues. Changing situations have led to new forms of religious life, new ministries and courageous acts of witness to the Gospel (including martyrdom) – surely a prophetic sign of life in the Church.

what is meant by 'eastern catholic churches?

The Eastern Catholic Churches are also known as 'Uniate Churches', that is, they are in union with Rome. They are separate from the Orthodox Churches, but they have retained their distinctive Eastern character.

uniate churches

There are six main 'rites':
Chaldean
Syrian
Melkite
Marconite
Coptic
Armenian
Byzantine.

The Ukrainian Church is part of the Byzantine rite.

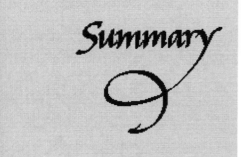

Summary

Decree on the Eastern Catholic Churches

(*Orientalium ecclesiarum* – OE)

INTRODUCTION

The Decree on the Eastern Catholic Churches is one of the shortest documents of the Council. It is essentially a Latin document about the Eastern Churches, but during the debate dissenting non-Latin voices were heard, notably that of the highly-respected Patriarch Maximos IV of the Melkite Church.

BACKGROUND

The Eastern Catholic Churches had a chequered history amid the confusions of the schism of Eastern and Western Christianity. Unfortunately, through cultural and linguistic difficulties, the Latin West imposed itself upon these ancient Churches. This Decree sought to redress this imbalance.

The Orthodox have always looked on the Eastern Catholic Churches with suspicion and dislike, as breaking up the unity of the East, by joining with Rome.

The Roman Catholic Church esteems the Eastern Catholic Churches, since they embody a tradition and a way of life that comes from apostolic times. Variety within the Church 'not only does no harm to its unity, but rather makes it manifest' (2).

The traditions of each individual Church are to be kept and adapted to time and place. All Churches enjoy equal dignity: they should each grow and develop throughout the world, and their spiritual heritage should be safeguarded. Patriarchs of the Eastern Churches have rights and privileges that are to be respected.

Eastern Churches in communion with Rome have special responsibility for furthering the unity of all Christians, especially Eastern Christians. The Decree encourages local Church dialogue concerning sacraments and celebrations, without prejudice to Rome.

The document finally looks to a coming together of all Christians, both Eastern and Western, in fuller union: 'Let us all love each other with the love of sisters and brothers, outdoing each other in showing honour' (Romans 12:10).

STRENGTHS

The Decree brought a welcome clarification of the position and rights of Eastern Catholic Churches. It expressed appreciation for them because they hold the traditions of the universal Church, in theology, spirituality and liturgy. They witness to the diversity of the Church and this witness continues to be important for the whole Church, in view of the increasing importance which became attached to local Churches, with their distinctive culture and traditions, as a result of the Second Vatican Council.

Moreover, ecumenically speaking, the Eastern Catholic Churches are recognised as a valuable link with the Orthodox Churches of Eastern Europe. Anglican Churches saw the strengthening of the position of the Uniate Churches as a sign of hope for the future.

LIMITATIONS

OE was only a beginning; problems regarding the position of these Churches continue. Neither side was in fact satisfied with this Decree. It left unclear the issue of the authority of the Holy See regarding these Churches. It did little to promote understanding between the Eastern Orthodox Churches and the Eastern Catholic Churches.

WHAT CAME NEXT?

This is a complex issue and it is difficult to attempt to evaluate significant observable changes. Some observers have noticed indications of helpful dialogue, for example, in India and parts of Eastern Europe. There is nevertheless a general feeling that the Decree is taking a long time to be implemented.

At the time, the Orthodox Churches welcomed the spirit of peace and goodwill of the Council, but with the political upheavals of the 1990s in Eastern Europe the world has seen a resurgence of antagonisms that had lain dormant.

questions on the document

1. Westerners see the Eastern Churches as exotic and different in their liturgy and customs. Does this dismay you or please you?

2. 'The strengths of the Eastern Catholic Churches lie in their ancient traditions and in their endurance through trials and stress.' What problems do they face today?

3. 'The significance of OE may lie in what the decree implies about the importance of the 'local Churches' which are in communion with Rome and with one another.' Do you agree?

If you are working in a group, take time:

TO SEE where we came from

TO UNDERSTAND the Decree

TO SHARE insights and responses

DISCUSS a possible way forward: where might we go from here?

MAKE a practical proposal or plan for the future.

Decree on Ecumenism

(*Unitatis redintegratio* – UR)

what is meant by 'ecumenism'?

Ecumenism is a desire to bring all Christians together into the unity for which Jesus prayed: 'May they all be one..' John. 17:21.

INTRODUCTION

This decree is one of the most important of the Council documents, next to the four Constitutions. It was originally intended to form part of LG. In calling the Council, Pope John XXIII stressed the ecumenical dimension of its purpose: 'to invite the separate communities to seek again that unity for which so many souls are longing in these days throughout the world'.

BACKGROUND

The 19th century Oxford Movement (led by John Keble, R.H. Froude and John Henry Newman) brought a revival and reappraisal of the early centuries of Church teaching among Anglican scholars. This opened the door for a return to earlier views on the nature of the Christian Church. Their work was further enhanced by the development of the study of history and by modern biblical studies in the Protestant Churches.

In 1910 at Edinburgh, there was an international conference which opened up the whole area of ecumenism. It was mainly concerned with the scandal of the rivalry among Christian missionaries. During the following forty years, many Churches moved, in relation to mission and social action, from respect for each other to cooperation at some level: they prayed together, and discussed organic unity. In 1948 the World Council of Churches (WCC) was formed as a result of decades of work among Protestant and Orthodox Churches.

The Roman Catholic Church distanced itself from this whole process. It took no part in any of the discussions or activities and did not join the WCC. However, there were some indications of concern for ecumenism. During 1921-1926 at Malines in Belgium, there were discussions about union with Anglican Churches. A priory was set up in which Catholic and Orthodox monks lived together in two parallel communities. The week of prayer for Christian unity, begun in 1909, attracted a degree of participation; yet a 1927 encyclical of Pope Pius XI spoke strongly against the ideas of the ecumenical movement. The official Catholic attitude remained aloof and sceptical: it represented, at best, a 'wait and see' policy.

Social and political changes in the 20th century were however moving the Churches towards greater awareness of views and ideas that had been hidden and unavailable. The controversies of the Reformation came to be studied and seen in a different light. Theologians tried to clarify and explain the differences between official teachings of different denominations and not just argue negatively about them. There was a movement away from denunciation and inquisition to communication and discussion. Ecumenism was seen to derive from the unifying inspiration of the Holy Spirit.

Theologians began to reflect on the nature of the Church and to develop a Catholic theology of unity. Rome gave permission in 1952 for the founding of a Catholic international conference for ecumenical questions.

In 1960 Pope John XXIII set up the Secretariat for Promoting Christian Unity, under Cardinal Bea and Cardinal Willebrands, and also sent observers to the WCC. Archbishop Fisher of Canterbury paid an historic visit to Pope John in the Vatican. This led to ecumenical observers being involved in preparatory work for the Council: they were also invited to the Council.

It is salutary to recall that, until the 1960s, Catholics were forbidden to pray with non-Catholics, or to attend funerals or other church services. The fact that this was taken for granted is an indication of what change the new attitudes of Vatican II would produce among ordinary Catholics.

Summary 9

that they all may be one. As you Father, are in me and I am in you, may they also be in us, so that the world may know that you have sent me and have loved them even as you have loved me.

John 17:21

Introduction

The first sentence of the Decree announces that 'the restoration of unity among all Christians is one of the principal concerns' of the Second Vatican Council. Division is understood to be contrary to Christ's will, and a scandal in the world. The modern ecumenical movement is seen as the work of the Holy Spirit.

Chapter 1: **Catholic principles of ecumenism**

Catholic principles of ecumenism follow from God's plan of salvation for the world, the saving mission of Christ, and the presence of the Holy Spirit in the Church. Christians separated from the Catholic Church belong to churches and communities used by the Spirit of Christ as a means of salvation. 'The people of God, though still in its members liable to sin, is growing in Christ during its pilgrimage on earth' (3).

The Council 'exhorts all the Catholic faithful to recognise the signs of the times and take an intelligent part in the work of ecumenism' (4).

Ecumenism is governed by three principles: unity in essentials, freedom and variety in non-essentials, and charity in all things (4). Catholics are invited to recognise the Holy Spirit in 'our separated brothers and sisters, as well as in our own Church'.

Chapter 2: **the practice of ecumenism**

Ecumenism is said to be linked closely with the renewal of the Church in various central spheres of its life. 'The restoration of unity is the concern of the whole Church, faithful and clergy alike. This concern extends to everyone according to their talents, whether it be exercised in ordinary Christian life or in theological and historical research' (5).

Moreover the Church is never perfect: 'in its pilgrimage on earth Christ summons the Church to continual reformation, of which it is always in need' (6).

Ecumenism affects the principle pastoral activities of the Church. It calls for a change of heart and for holiness of life. Catholics are invited to pray for the unity of the Church, sometimes with other Christians.

Theological study and dialogue with other Christians will help Catholics to 'get to know the outlook of our separated fellow Christians'. Ecumenical meetings for discussion of theological problems are seen as most valuable: 'where each side can treat with the other on equal footing, provided that those who take part in them under the guidance of their authorities are truly competent' (9).

Faith and doctrine must be expressed clearly but explained profoundly and precisely, so that non-Catholic Christians can understand. Catholic theologians are invited to study theology with other Christians 'with love for the truth, with charity and with humility' (11).

Catholic theologians are reminded that 'in Catholic doctrine there exists an order or hierarchy of truths, since they vary in their connection with the foundation of Christian faith' (11). This observation was to be regarded as an important principle in the renewal of Catholic theology after Vatican II.

Chapter 3: churches and ecclesial communities separated from the Roman apostolic see

Ecclesial communities separated from the Roman Church include two main groups: _Eastern Churches_, divided among themselves as a result of disputes after the Councils of Ephesus and Chalcedon (451 AD), and separated from the west in the Great Schism (1054 AD); _Protestant Churches_ separated from the See of Rome at the time of the sixteenth-century Reformation, among which is the Anglican communion to which UR allocates a special place(13).

Eastern Churches contain a treasury of liturgical prayer and spiritual life, 'Far from being an obstacle to the Church's unity, a certain diversity of customs and observances only adds to her beauty and is of great help in carrying out her mission' (16).

Protestant Churches and ecclesial communities differ in several important ways from the Catholic Church, including differences in 'the interpreting of revealed truth', but they 'look to Christ as the source and centre of ecclesiastical communion' (20) and are marked by a love and reverence for holy Scripture. Despite 'considerable divergences' in doctrine, these Churches share a sacramental bond of unity with Catholics through baptism.

The ecumenical movement is invited to discuss the application of the Gospel to 'the more difficult problems of modern society' (24), and to seek unity prayerfully in a spirit of hope, as the gift of God's Spirit.

ecumenical milestones

1 The Franciscan Friars and Sisters of the Atonement were founded in 1898 at Graymoor, New York, by Fr Paul Wattson and Mother Mary Lurana White, both Episcopalians. The whole Graymoor community of seventeen was received corporately into the Roman Catholic Church in 1909.

• Also in 1909, Fr Wattson inaugurated an eight-day period of prayer called the Church Unity Octave, beginning on the feast of St Peter's Chair (18 January) and finishing on the Conversion of St Paul (25 January). This is now universally celebrated by Churches as an annual period of ecumenical prayer and action.

2 The Corymeela Community in Northern Ireland was founded in 1965.

It is an inter-denominational Christian community which seeks to promote reconciliation in the troubled society from which it has grown.

STRENGTHS

The decree has been seen as the charter for participation of Catholics in the ecumenical movement. As a result of the decree and actions of the Council, the Catholic Church now takes part in the one great movement to bring about the unity of the Church.

The ecumenical movement was relatively new, and the decree was an affirmation of the Holy Spirit moving and guiding the Church. As Cardinal Bea said, 'No one will tell us, 'we did it this way last time!'

Respect for other Churches

These are no longer referred to as sects but as churches or ecclesial communities. Christian communities are seen to follow in the footsteps of the apostles and to work for the coming of the Kingdom. Since this is not yet achieved, no community is perfect: each is in need of purification and reform.

What we have in common is our following of Christ, the same Scriptures as the basis of life, and our life in community. We are therefore encouraged to pray together and work together whenever possible.

Doctrine

• The concept of a hierarchy of truths provides a starting point for evaluating doctrines and for considering differences: some truths are closer to the central mystery of faith than others.

• It is accepted that doctrine and liturgy are not limited to the ways of thinking of the Latin West.

• Dialogue with other Churches is to be on equal footing, with no assumption of moral superiority.

• Priests and pastoral ministers are encouraged to develop a non-polemical theology, seeking understanding rather than confrontation, and discussion rather than divisive argument.

• The 'special place' allotted to the Anglican communion in relation to its Catholic traditions and institutions was felt to be encouraging.

LIMITATIONS

Since this was the first major Roman effort to consider this topic, it was necessarily somewhat tentative because of the need to seek consensus and a way forward. Inherited patterns of separation and suspicion are not easily overcome and, at times, this is evident from the document's tentative wording. Underlying issues remain to be clarified and there are some ambiguities in the language used concerning the Protestant Churches.

WHAT CAME NEXT?

The impact of ecumenical enthusiasm went beyond the Decree, and UR became a major point of reference for Church renewal throughout other documents of Vatican II, for instance AG. The rapidity with which UR assumed its place as a vital part of the life of the Catholic Church inside the Council and in many countries attests to its significance. However, it has also been described as a mixture of high hopes and dashed promises. In 1987 Cardinal Willebrands spoke of the dialogue which followed the Council as 'a new context in the making', which was by no means completed.

These were only the early stages of ecumenism in the Catholic Church. For many people, authentic ecumenical thinking is very foreign. This is hardly surprising. The decree was not expressing in words what was already happening but pointing out a new way forward. It was truly an innovation and as such requires time to percolate into minds and hearts at all levels in the Church. It began a new tradition, which, in spite of disappointments, is irresistible and irrevocable.

Since the Council there has been a great range of ecumenical activity, official and unofficial, at parish, national and world levels, astonishing in its variety. It must also be said that many Christians feel that, thirty years after Vatican II, the ecumenical movement has lost much of its impetus, so that some enthusiasts for ecumenism go so far as to talk about an 'ecumenical winter' having invaded the Roman Church.

Ecumenical dialogues, internationally as well as nationally, were opened up after the Council, with almost all the Protestant Churches of the Reformation. Moreover, ecumenical gestures have become commonplace in the mass media, in public meetings, and in exchanges of visits by Church leaders.

ecumenical milestones

Surprising things happened which had not been envisaged by the Council. No-one could have predicted the pace of development of awareness between the Churches. Much dialogue takes place locally, to a degree not envisaged by Church leaders.

Important developments in the Churches have overtaken the agenda for unity envisioned at Vatican II. By 1985 sixty per cent of the bishops in the World Synod were not from Europe. They were concerned with the new debates about world poverty, justice, inculturation and environmental issues in view of the needs of the young Churches. Another factor has been the rapid growth of evangelical and charismatic Churches since the 1960s, as well as the fundamentalist groups that have gained ground and which make the ecumenical problem even more difficult to resolve.

Nevertheless the impetus to work together with other Churches that flowed from the Council remains impressive. The two bishops of Liverpool. Archbishop Derek Worlock and Bishop David Shepherd, have set a welcome example, as have the ecumenical communities of Taize, Iona and Corymeela, as well as numerous other examples of Christian sharing which are less well-known. (see *Ecumenical Milestones* pp. 86, 88)

Meanwhile, the pain of division, keenly felt, continues to be a scandal to the non-Christian world.

RELATIONS BETWEEN ROMAN CATHOLICS AND ANGLICANS

These have been developed at an official level through ARCIC (Anglican Roman Catholic International Commission): ARCIC I, 1970-1981, inspired by Pope Paul VI; ARCIC II, 1982-, created by Pope John Paul II and Archbishop Runcie, following the papal visit to Great Britain.

Four Statements were agreed by ARCIC I: Eucharistic Doctrine (Windsor 1971); Ministry and Ordination (Canterbury 1973); Authority in the Church I (Venice 1976) and II (Windsor 1981).

A 'final report' of agreements and elucidations was drawn up and submitted in 1981, but it received a rather negative reaction from the (Roman) Congregation for the

Doctrine of the Faith. ARCIC II was established in 1982 to continue the study of doctrinal difficulties and to recommend practical steps with a view towards full communion between the Churches. Discussions about the Roman recognition of the validity of Anglican orders (declared to be invalid by Pope Leo XIII) are still in progress. The decision of the Anglican Church in England to ordain women priests brought a crisis for some Anglican clergy and lay people who were led to become Roman Catholics.

RELATIONS BETWEEN ROMAN CATHOLICS AND OTHER CHRISTIANS

• The question of inter-communion continues to be a live issue. In general, Roman Catholics may not welcome others to communion nor may they take communion in other churches, although local bishops have discretion, in certain circumstances, to allow other Christians to receive communion in the Catholic Church. This lack of unity sometimes inhibits communal worship.

• The discipline surrounding marriage between Catholics and other Christians is an important practical issue. To marry a Christian of another Church no longer requires a dispensation, although to marry an unbaptised person does. The promise to bring up the children as Catholics is no longer required of non-Catholics; this is seen to be the responsibility of the Catholic partner.

• In 1990, a milestone was reached when the Roman Catholic Church entered into full membership of the Council of Churches for Britain and Ireland (CCBI). Speaking at the first full meeting of Churches Together in England (CTE), Cardinal Hume said: "Spirituality, social action and education are, for me, priorities which we can and should try to address together."

questions on the document

1. 'In its pilgrimage on earth, Christ summons the Church to continual reformation, of which it is always in need, in so far as it is an institution of human beings here on earth' (UR6). This teaching is at the centre of the decree on ecumenism. Do you agree? If so, why?

2. Why did Vatican II consider ecumenism to be important? Point out some practical ecumenical developments which have affected the local Church since Vatican II?

3. Are you aware of the life and beliefs of other Christians in your locality? Have they influenced you in any way?

If you are working in a group, take time:

TO SEE where we came from

TO UNDERSTAND the Decree

TO SHARE insights and responses

DISCUSS a possible way forward: where might we go from here?

MAKE a practical proposal or plan for the future.

Decree on the Missionary Activity of the Church

(*Ad gentes* – AG)

what is meant by 'missionary activity'?

The word 'mission' means sending. God sends missionaries across human frontiers to proclaim the good news of the Kingdom, to offer God's love through service, dialogue and liberation, and to build up a community of shared life in Christ. Through the work of missionaries, local Churches already established reach out to one another in mutual ministry, supporting one another.

INTRODUCTION

Missionary activity has been part of the Church since earliest times, but in the 1960s its purpose and value needed to be reassessed. The world had changed rapidly in the twentieth century, and Vatican II was the first Council to have representatives from the vast missionary areas of the world. The position of 'young Churches' was critical in the re-thinking of the theology of the universal Church.

In the past, some missionary activity had been marred by both a lack of awareness and a lack of respect for the grace of God to be found in the values of non-European cultures and religions, and by the competitive rivalries of various Christian missionaries. AG was intended to help Catholics move away from a narrow sectarianism, and to guide missionaries in their work of evangelisation by helping them to look positively at different cultures.The Decree begins:

'At the present time, when a new era for humanity is emerging, the Church, salt of the earth and light of the world, is called with greater energy to strive for the salvation and renewal of every human being, so that everything may be restored in Christ and that in him all humankind may form but one family and one people of God' (1).

BACKGROUND

During the one hundred years before Vatican II, the world was dominated by European colonial cultures, which encouraged a great deal of overseas missionary activity. Between 1919 and 1959 Popes published five encyclical letters about the missions. The tendency in the Church was to see the world from a European perspective, making sharp distinctions between overseas 'missions' and long-established European Churches. Moreover, in colonial days, the Church's missionary activity was characterised by clericalism and paternalism, with little place for real dialogue with the people concerned. After the Second World

War, radical changes in the world meant that many colonial countries obtained independence, while the new ecumenical era was also seen to offer opportunities to replace scandalous rivalries between Christian missionaries with co-operation. The time was ripe for a newly thought-out theology of 'the missions' with very practical implications.

It proved difficult to write this Decree, because of disagreements about its content and style. Eventually, between the third and final sessions of the Council, a new draft was drawn up by bishops and theologians with missionary experience. AG builds on the strengths of the *Constitution on the Church* and the then still-evolving *Pastoral Constitution on the Church in the World of Today*. Many of those who wrote the new decree had taken part in the important international Pan-African Catechetical Seminar at Katigondo, Uganda, in August 1964, in which particular attention had been paid to the religious and cultural outlook of Africans.

Summary

God made all nations.."so that they would search for God and perhaps grope for him and find him - though indeed he is not far from each of us. For 'in him we live and more and have our being'...

Acts 17:27-28

Chapter 1: **doctrinal principles.**

'The pilgrim church is of its very nature missionary, since it draws its origin from the mission of the Son and the mission of the Holy Spirit, in accordance with the plan of God the Father' (1).

The opening paragraphs develop the theological implications of the Church's very existence, reminding Catholics about why the Church exists and of the importance of its mission in God's plan of salvation. This implies following in the footsteps of Christ along 'a road of poverty, obedience, service and self-sacrifice' (5).

The Church's mission is also linked to the ecumenical movement, 'for the division among Christians damages the holy work of preaching the Gospel to every creature' (5). 'The Church has both the obligation and the sacred right to evangelise' (7), so missionary activity remains necessary in today's world.

Chapter 2: **missionary work itself**

More than two billion people have still to hear the Gospel message. The Church's missionary task is accomplished by Christian witness. Christ's faithful should associate with the non-Christians in their midst 'in a spirit of respect and love... they should be familiar with their national and religious traditions; they should with joy and reverence discover the seeds of the Word which lie hidden in them' (11).

The presence of Christians should be marked by charity which reaches out to all, 'without distinction of race, social condition or religion', which affects even the social and economic aspects of life (12).

Non-Christians are converted by a gradual process, a 'spiritual journey' of Christian initiation during the catechumenate which involves the entire community of the faithful (14).

As fellow workers with the Holy Spirit, missionaries form Christian communities, able to cater for their own needs (15), with a sense of mission, and with various ministries and vocations: lay Christians, priests, deacons, catechists and religious.

Chapter 3: concerning particular churches

There is more to establishing a Church than planting a seed: 'In these young churches, the life of the people of God ought to mature... to become living communities of faith' with their own liturgy, culture and pastoral dedication (19).

The principle of the Incarnation means it is important to search for faith to be expressed in ways appropriate to local culture (22).

Chapter 4: missionaries

The Lord stirs up individual missionaries and missionary institutes to be Christ-like ministers of the Gospel. Future missionaries should be prepared by a special spiritual and moral formation (25), e.g. in missionary institutes.

Chapter 5: the organisation of missionary activity

Missionary effort needs to be co-ordinated by the Congregation for the Propagation of the Faith - searching (with the aid of the Secretariat for the Promotion of Christian Unity) for co-operation with other Christian communities. 'All who work in the missions should have 'one heart and one mind' (30), working in cooperation with the local bishop and his pastoral council.

Different missionary institutes are called to work with 'friendly and generous collaboration' (34).

Chapter 6: co-operation

'Since the entire Church is missionary and the spreading of the Gospel is a fundamental duty of the people of God', the Council invites everyone to a profound interior renewal, so they can become 'the light of the world' and 'the salt of the earth' (Matthew 5). All Catholics are called to devote their energies to the work of evangelisation. Episcopal conferences should co-ordinate missionary efforts. Different members of the Church community are specified and encouraged to become actively involved.

And he said to them, 'Go into all the world and proclaim the good news to the whole creation'.
Mark 16:15

STRENGTHS

• The major emphasis of AG is that the whole Church is missionary by divine calling: its activity includes missionary evangelisation among all nations, pastoral work among believers, and fostering ecumenical relations with other Christians. All Christians – not just priests and religious – are called to be missionary. Every local Church is called to be a 'living community of faith, of liturgy and of charity' (19).

• AG recognises that the Christian faith needs to be proclaimed and lived in a pluralistic world whose cultural values are predominantly non-Christian. A great strength of the Decree is the value it recognises in different human cultures (22), in which 'seeds of the Word' lie hidden (11). The focus of AG is on the active presence of the Church within diverse cultures rather than on territorial expansion of the European Church. AG's teaching is relevant to such themes as the need to adapt expressions of faith to local conditions, participation in community and national life, co-operation between different Christian communities and dialogue with non-Christians.

• AG emphasises the central place of conversion in Christian life. Its treatment of the catechumenate as 'a training in the entire Christian life... an apprenticeship by which the disciples are drawn close to Christ their master' (14) uses the missionary experience of Christian initiation to develop the implications of SC 64's restoration of the catechumenate to the universal Church.

LIMITATIONS

• The theology of AG is now seen to be marked by certain unresolved inconsistencies: for example, sometimes missionary activity is centred on proclaiming Christ, at other times on establishing the institutional Church.

• AG suggests a picture of a mature European or North American Church sending out missionaries to evangelise the Third World which lacks structures and resources. Thirty years after Vatican II, western Churches are in a state of decline and weakness, lacking vocations to priesthood and religious life. Local Churches can no longer be divided into 'sending' and 'receiving' Churches, and indeed mission today can be said to be multi-directional. Not only are Europe and North America seen as valid missionary contexts, but all local Churches are potentially mission sending and mission receiving. This is attested by the actual geography of missionary recruitment and destination. A 'new evangelisation' is seen to be necessary in traditionally Christian countries, which was not foreseen in AG.

WHAT CAME NEXT?

• Developments from AG fed into a profound change of attitude and priorities whereby the Church rediscovered her mission to be on the side of (or to take a preferential option for) the poor.

• Study of traditional religions and cultures was promoted by this Decree. It has become important in the education of all missionaries. In his journeys, Pope John Paul II has emphasised the importance of 'inculturation' of the Gospel in every type of society. A picture emerges of a communion of Churches in different cultures, enriching one another and giving new expression to the Gospel through such inculturation. In several Latin American countries, the Council's teaching and the theological developments which followed have produced nothing short of a revolution. 'Basic communities' have transformed the life of the Church.

These profound changes do not conform to any process envisaged by AG. The tensions between these lively new communities and the old structures of hierarchically-defined mission are acutely felt in some local Churches.

In 1975, Pope Paul VI's apostolic exhortation on Evangelisation (*Evangelii Nuntiandi*) was published, following the 1974 Synod on Evangelisation. This came to be recognised as a key document in the post-conciliar Church. It presents its teaching in detailed sections on 'From Christ the Evangeliser to the Evangelising Church', 'What is Evangelisation?', 'The Message of Evangelisation', 'The Means of Evangelisation', 'The Universality of Evangelisation', 'The Evangelisers', and 'The Spirit of Evangelisation'.

Pope Paul insisted that evangelisation was 'the function and duty imposed on the Church by Our Lord Jesus Christ so that all may believe and achieve salvation' (5): 'Evangelisation is the special grace and vocation of the Church. It is her essential function.' (14).

• Lay missionaries have broken the mold of what was thought of as 'missionary'. So has the growth of

questions on the document

1.'The entire Church is missionary'. Why does the Church exist? What is its mission?

2. 'A great strength of AG is the value it recognises in different human cultures.' Why is it important that Christian missionaries respect the native culture of the people to whom they are sent?

3. What problems would Christian missionaries expect to meet in this country?

4. How might the Church's missionary task be accomplished in this country?

If you are working in a group, take time:

TO SEE where we came from

TO UNDERSTAND the Decree

TO SHARE insights and responses

DISCUSS a possible way forward: where might we go from here?

MAKE a practical proposal or plan for the future.

international development agencies like CAFOD (the Catholic Fund for Overseas Development established by the bishops of England and Wales in 1962). CAFOD sees its work in terms of a partnership between Catholics in this country and communities in Latin America, Asia and Africa. CAFOD funds over 700 projects in 75 countries. It also responds to emergency needs of crisis victims. Funds are raised through parish groups, school activities, special fund-raising events and government grants. At the same time, through its imaginative educational literature, CAFOD promotes an understanding of under-development and its underlying causes, and is thus committed to educating and evangelising the home Church.

• Now the tide of missionary activity is starting to flow from other directions. Those countries that were 'missions' are now themselves evangelising other places, even Europe.

• The task of dialogue with other faiths is no longer an option but a necessity for world order. (See the treatment of Vatican II's *Declaration on the Relation of the Church to non-Christian Religions* (NA) p.119 ff.)

• A traditional understanding of the Church's missionary activity as evangelisation remains important, fostered by the Association for the Propagation of the Faith (APF), founded by Pauline Jaricot in 1822. The 1990s were named by Pope John Paul II as a 'decade of new evangelisation' and inaugurated by his encyclical *The Mission of the Redeemer* (Redemptoris Missio, 1990), written to commemorate the 25th anniversary of AG and to renew the urgency of missionary activity in the Church.

The Pope writes: "Today, as never before, the Church has the opportunity of bringing the Gospel, by witness and word, to all people and nations. I see the dawning of a new missionary age, which will become an abundant harvest, if all Christians, and missionaries and young Churches in particular, respond with generosity and holiness to the calls and challenges of our time" (92).

Focus on the Church in the World of Today

In its Pastoral Constitution on the Church in the World of Today (Gaudium et Spes), Vatican II addresses all people, inviting them 'to contribute to discovering a solution to the outstanding questions of our day'.

We group three related documents with this Constitution. These open up a number of typically modern questions about the world of our time.

They are:
the Decree on the Mass Media (Inter mirifica)
the Declaration on Religious Freedom (Dignitatis humanae)
the Declaration on the Relationship of the Church to non-Christian Religions (Nostra aetate)

Pastoral Constitution on the Church in the World of Today (*Gaudium et Spes* – GS)

why look at 'the church in the world of today'?

GS examines the link between the Church and world today. Instead of the world being described negatively as a place of sin, the Council describes it as the 'stage of human history..... kept in being by its Creator's love' (GS 2).

"It is only in freedom, however, that human beings can turn to what is good, and our contemporaries are right in their assiduous pursuit of such freedom, although often they cultivate it in wrong ways as a licence to do anything they please (17)".

INTRODUCTION

Vatican II's last, longest and most complex document is for many people its most stimulating achievement, notable for its wide range of concerns. This complex document is made easier to read because each numbered section has a sub-title indicating its content; these sign-posts enable readers to follow the overall direction of the text or to look up specific topics. (You may wish to do so, especially in relation to topics contained in part 2, and not discussed in detail here.)

The document is in two distinct parts, described in its own words as follows: 'In the first part the Church develops its doctrine about humanity, the world in which human beings live, and its relationship to both. The second concentrates on several aspects of modern living and human society, and specifically on questions and problems which seem particularly urgent today. As a result, this latter part comprises material, subject to doctrinal considerations, which contains both permanent and transient features.'

BACKGROUND

GS's background contrasts with the movements which led up to the other three constitutions of the Council. There was no movement like the Biblical or Liturgical movements to prepare the way for this Constitution, except the tradition since 1891 of papal social encyclicals. GS's origins lie rather in a diffuse but growing sense that the Church had to find new ways of addressing the world of today.

The immediate impetus came from Cardinal Suenens. At the end of the first session in December 1962, he asked that the Council express not only the nature of the Church's inner reality but also its relationship with the contemporary world. No preliminary text had been prepared as this was not part of the original agenda of the Council. It would take the remaining three years and much passionate debate to arrive at an agreed text, a text finally approved on the last working day of the Council in December 1965.

A draft produced in 1963 stressed the absolute moral order, with timeless principles expressed as abstract concepts. Some bishops and lay consultants asked for a bolder and more concrete approach to practical moral problems. Two papal actions during the Council set precedents supporting this bolder approach.

'To all people of good will'

In 1963 Pope John issued his encyclical *Peace on Earth.* It built on the social teaching of the Church, teaching which had first addressed the moral problems of industrialised society in Pope Leo XIII's encyclical *Rerum Novarum* in 1891. Subsequent Popes had developed this further to offer Catholic insights on the growing number of issues raised by modern economic systems.

[handwritten: 1st encyclical addressed to all ppl of good will = not just Catholic]

Pope John now broadened the scope of this teaching. His was the first papal encyclical addressed not only to Catholics but also 'to all people of good will'. Furthermore, it was the first to link economic under-development to disarmament. This prophetic statement was one of Pope John's final acts before he died.

Pope Paul followed this in 1965 with the first papal visit to the United Nations, during which he made an impassioned plea for aid for the less developed nations and an end to war. His ratification of the UN was heard as the voice of a rejuvenated Church keen to enter into the main stream of human affairs. This was no longer a Church in opposition to modernity but a Church committed to dialogue with the modern world.

[handwritten: UN participation by Vatican]

Emboldened by this background, GS was addressed to 'people everywhere' and took a global view of issues facing humanity today. It developed the papal teaching on economic issues and also underlined recent teaching on disarmament. It went further than this, however, by offering an in-depth analysis of modern attitudes and modern culture, using insights drawn from psychology and sociology. All of this was then set within the context of Scripture rather than the customary Catholic basis for social morality which was the philosophy of natural law.

GS was the fruit of profound and lengthy dialogue between bishops, theological advisers and secular experts. Pope Paul himself was instrumental in supporting this document through its many difficulties.

Out of this ferment of searching there emerged a document less polished than others. Its treatment of some issues is incomplete, so that one cannot simply apply its teaching as if it were a manual of instructions. It is, however, unique in the history of the Church. It is the only statement of any ecumenical council that deals not with issues of Church order and doctrine but with the practicalities of life in the world.

The Church has the duty
in every age of examining the
signs of the times
and interpreting them
in the light of the Gospel
GS:4

Preface: The close link between the Church and the whole human family

The joys and hopes and the sorrows and anxieties of people today, especially of the poor and afflicted, are also the joys and hopes, sorrows and anxieties of the disciples of Christ, and there is nothing truly human which does not affect them (1).

Introduction: The condition of humanity in today's world.

The Church has the duty in every age of examining the signs of the times and interpreting them in the light of the Gospel. The human race finds itself today in a new stage of its history, in which fundamental and rapid changes are gradually extending to the whole globe (4).

The spiritual unease of today and the change in living conditions are part of a greater upheaval. The human race is moving from a static view of things to one which is more dynamic and evolutionary (5).

The industrial type of society is spreading, leading some nations to economic wealth and utterly transforming age-old ideas and conditions of social living (6).

A change in mentality and structures is frequently challenging traditional values, especially on the part of the young who are at times impatient, if not in revolt. The result is that parents and teachers find their tasks increasingly difficult (7).

Imbalances arise between races and various classes of society; between rich nations and the weaker and more needy ones (8).

Considerable numbers insistently demand those advantages of which they feel very conscious of being deprived. For the first time in human history, whole peoples are convinced that the benefits of culture really can and should extend to everyone (9). An increasing number are asking: What is the human person? (10).

PART ONE: The Church and humanity's vocation
1. The dignity of the human person

Everything on earth is to be referred to humanity as its centre and culmination. Although constituted in righteousness by God, the human being is divided interiorly, and the whole of human life, whether singly or shared, is shown to be a dramatic struggle between good and evil (13).

...for God created us for incorruption, and made us in the image of his own eternity,

Wisdom 2: 23

Deep within their conscience individuals discover a law which they do not make for themselves but which they are bound to obey, whose voice, ever summoning them to love and do what is good and to avoid evil, rings in their heart: Do this, keep away from that. (16).

It is only in freedom, however, that human beings can turn to what is good, and our contemporaries are right in their assiduous pursuit of such freedom, although often they cultivate it in wrong ways as a licence to do anything they please (17). The outstanding feature of human dignity is that human beings are called to communion with God. Many of our contemporaries, however, refuse to accept this relationship (19).

One form of atheism looks towards people's economic and social liberation and claims that religion is an obstacle to such liberation in raising people's hopes towards a future illusory life which would discourage them from building the earthly city (20).

The message of the Church is, however, in harmony with the deepest desires of the human heart. Far from diminishing humankind, this message spreads light, life and liberty (21). In fact, it is only in the mystery of the Word incarnate that light is shed on the mystery of humankind (22).

2. The human community

Love for God cannot be separated from love for neighbour (24).

Everything should be rendered to a person which is required to lead a truly human life - food, clothing, shelter, the rights to freedom, education, work and respect (26).

Whatever is hostile to life itself (homicide, genocide, abortion, euthanasia); whatever is offensive to human dignity (arbitrary imprisonment, slavery, prostitution): all these and the like are a disgrace (27).

Although there are just differences among individuals, the excessive inequalities among peoples are a scandal at variance with social justice and international peace (29). No one should, through disregard for events or lethargy, indulge in a merely individualist morality. There are some people who are bountiful and generous in their views but who behave in fact as if they had no care for society's needs.

For you did not receive a spirit of slavery to fall back into fear, but you have received a spirit of adoption. When we cry, 'Abba! Father' it is that very Spirit bearing witness with our spirit that we are children of God...
Romans 8:15-16

Social relationships are among the most important responsibilities of all of us today (30). Education needs to be undertaken in such a way that it produces people who are not just cultivated but also generous.

The future of humanity is in the hands of those who can hand on to posterity grounds for living and for hope (31). God did not create human beings to live separately but to form a united society (32).

3. Human activity throughout the world

Created in God's image, humankind was commissioned to subdue the earth and all it contains, to rule the world in justice and holiness. The successes of the human race are a sign of God's greatness and marvellous design (34).

If we take the autonomy of earthly realities to mean that created things and societies have their own laws and values which are to be gradually discovered, utilised and ordered by us, then it is perfectly proper to claim such autonomy. Therefore, methodical inquiry in all disciplines can never really be at variance with faith, since secular realities and the realities of faith have their origin in the same God (36).

Yet Christians proclaim that all human activity, which is daily jeopardised through pride and distorted self-love, needs to be purified and completed by the cross and resurrection of Christ (37).

4. The Church's task in today's world

The Church believes that, through its individual members and as a whole, it can contribute to making the human family and its history more human (40).

No human law is as able to safeguard the personal dignity and freedom of humans as fittingly as the Gospel which Christ has entrusted to his Church (41).

The particular mission which Christ entrusted to his Church is of a religious nature, yet this mission produces a function, enlightenment and resources which can be of service in constructing and strengthening the human community (42).

The split between the faith which they profess and the daily lives of many people is to be counted as among the more serious misconceptions of our day. No false opposition should be set up between professional and social activities on the one hand and the life of religion on the other. The

Mission of church in World

summary

→ next page

God saw everything that he had made, and indeed, it was very good.

Genesis 1: 31

laity may expect enlightenment and spiritual help from the clergy, but they should not consider that their pastors have the expertise needed to provide a concrete and ready answer to every problem which arises, even the most serious ones. The laity have their own part to play (43).

While it helps the world and receives much from the world, the Church has only one goal, namely the coming of God's Kingdom and the accomplishment of salvation for the whole human race (45).

what is this

PART TWO: Some urgent problems

Having outlined the dignity of the human person and the individual and social task which we are called to fulfil in the world as a whole, the Council now draws attention in the light of the Gospel and of human experience, to certain urgent contemporary needs which particularly affect the human race (46). Instead of a summary for this lengthy section of the document, we list the titles of the various paragraphs of GS and offer a specimen quotation from each chapter. This indicates the scope of this document. Readers may then wish to turn to the document for further study.

Chapter 1: promoting the dignity of marriage and the family

47. Marriage and the family in the modern world

48. The holiness of marriage and the family

49. Married love

50. The fruitfulness of marriage

51. Reconciling married love with respect for human life

52. Promoting marriage and the family as the concern of all

Chapter 2: the proper development of culture
Introduction

53. **Section 1:** the conditions of culture in today's world

54. New forms of living

55. Man and woman as the authors of culture

56. Difficulties and duties

Section 2: some principles for the proper development of culture.

57. Faith and culture

58. Multiple connections between the good news of Christ and human culture

59. The proper relationships between different forms of human culture

Section 3: some urgent tasks for Christians affecting culture

60. The rights to the benefits of culture should be recognised and implemented for all

61. Education for a completely human culture

62. The correct relationship between human and social culture and Christian formation

family

The family is a school for a richer humanity. For it to find fulfilment in its life and mission, it needs openness and cooperation on the part of husband and wife and their committed cooperation in raising their children... Children should be educated in such a way that on reaching adulthood, they can exercise full responsibility in following their calling... and in choosing a way of life in which, if they marry, they can found their own family under suitable moral, social and economic conditions. It is for parents or educators to act as guides to young people establishing a family, by their prudent advice which should be willingly listened to. (52)

culture

Christ's faithful on pilgrimage to a heavenly city should seek and value what is above; but far from diminishing, this enhances the importance of their duty to collaborate with all others in building a world of more human construction. In fact, the mystery of the Christian faith provides them with greater incentive and help in fulfilling this task more enthusiastically, and especially in uncovering the full significance of the work, according human culture its distinguished place in the complete vocation of humankind. (57)

socio-economics

God has destined the earth and all it contains for the use of everyone and of all peoples, so that the good things of creation should be available equally to all, with justice as guide and charity in attendance... For this reason, in making use of them, we ought to regard the exterior things we lawfully possess not just as our own but also as common, in the sense that they can profit not only the owners but others also... 'Feed those who are dying of hunger, because if you have not fed them you have killed them.' (69)

political community

Citizens should generously and faithfully practise loyalty to their own country, but without narrow-mindedness, and should always at the same time look to the good of the entire human family which is united by various connections between races, peoples and nations. (75)

war

It must be stated once more that the arms race is a virulent plague affecting humanity and that it does intolerable harm to the poor. And if it continues, then it is greatly to be feared that at some time it will produce all the deadly disasters for which it is now preparing the means... God's providence urgently expects us to free ourselves from the age-old slavery to war. If we decline to make this attempt, we do not know the outcome of this wrong path on which we have set foot... It is therefore evident that we must struggle to use all our resources to create a time when nations can agree to a complete ban on all war (81-82).

peace

Christians can have nothing more at heart than to be of ever more generous service to humanity in the modern world. That is why, in fidelity to the Gospel and drawing on its power, and in union with all who love and pursue justice, they have accepted a vast undertaking on this earth, for which they will have to render an account to the God who will judge everyone on the last day. Not all who say 'Lord, Lord', will enter the Kingdom but those who do the will of the Father and put a strong hand to the task (93).

STRENGTHS

Among the many strengths of GS, we highlight four:

• The signs of the times are seen as the starting point for reflecting on the Church's mission to the world. The Church does not stand at a distance but sees itself as part of the historic forces at work in our rapidly changing world. The task is to interpret these forces for change not simply to condemn them because they are new.

In this changing world, the Church recognises that questioning and searching are the norm in modern life. The tone is one of seeking and listening: 'in a time characterised by rapid change and a growing variety in ways of thought, the Church has particular need of those who live in the world, whether they are believers or not, and who are familiar with its various institutions and disciplines. It is for God's people as a whole to listen to the various voices of our day, discerning them and interpreting them, and to evaluate them in the light of the divine word, so that the revealed truth can be increasingly appropriated, better understood and more suitably expressed' (44). GS is itself full of questions.

• Atheism is recognised as an aspect of the modern world, a part not only to be deplored but also to be understood and listened to. Some bishops asked that atheistic communism be specifically condemned but the majority felt that such condemnation was not in the spirit of the Council. Indeed, the Church takes responsibility for sometimes causing atheism through 'believers who may be described more as concealing the true features of God and religion than as revealing them' (19).

• Intellectual freedom of research is commended. Scientists and thinkers are free to pursue research, provided they do nothing immoral.

There was discussion about the fate of the 16th century scientist, Galileo, who had been silenced by the Church for the results of his research into the nature of motion, in particular the motion of the planets. He had concluded that the earth was not the centre of the universe and that the medieval Church's view of God sending energy down to earth through the heavens was misguided. 'One can legitimately regret attitudes to be found sometimes even among Christians... which have led many people to conclude from the disagreements and controversies which such attitudes have aroused, that there is opposition between faith and science' (36). To this statement is added a footnote referring to a modern biography of Galileo by an author whose work had recently been prevented from publication by the Church. In a symbolic gesture in 1990, Pope John Paul II was to revoke the Church's condemnation of Galileo.

• In Part Two, there are significant developments in the Church's moral teaching, stating clearly and in an authoritative way convictions that had been emerging about family life, property and war.

In the section on family life, mutual love between the partners and raising children are both affirmed as the aims of marriage, but the whole tone is one of affirming and celebrating the fulfilment of the whole person through married life, not just raising children.

In the section on socio-economic life, there is the traditional Catholic respect for private property but strongly tempered by a lively awareness of the common good; this awareness is essential to Christian living and must express itself in action on behalf of those in need.

In the section on war, the right to self-defence is affirmed but the condemnation of the use of weapons of mass destruction is clearly stated; this led some members of the Council (e.g. Abbot Christopher Butler) to conclude that even the possession of nuclear weapons was immoral, on the grounds that the intention to use was as bad as actually using such weapons.

o Ways to engage in new challenges of the world.

o How to get aid to poor? What governments are okay? A neutral position given.

109

various influences can be seen in CWT

• *Cardinal Cardijn (founder of the Young Christian Workers) asked that attention be given to the concerns of the young, the working classes and the Third World.*

• *Cardinal Konig (president of the newly formed Secretariat for Unbelievers) wanted to emphasise the different kinds of atheism and to encouraging dialogue without compromising faith.*

• *Lay advisers pressed for more about marriage and family life but the Pope reserved the issue of contraception to a special papal commission which would report after the Council. From among lay advisers on world development including Barbara Ward from Britain, James Norris from the USA was asked to address the Council; he urged that richer countries had an obligation to create a more just world.*

• *Observers from the World Council of Churches suggested emphasising the Lordship of the Risen Christ over Church and world based on Scripture.*

• *Father Chenu was central in encouraging a return to Scripture and the sources of faith, to accompany the interpretation of the signs of the times. The influence of other French theologians is seen in the document's concern with the evangelisation of culture, a particular concern in France whose secular culture had led to France being declared a mission country in 1945.*

LIMITATIONS

For all its strengths, GS is not without its weaknesses. Some of these stem from its broad scope and its practical nature. The breadth of the whole document means that the two parts are quite distinct, almost separate statements. The practicality of part two means that some sections are now out of date, while other issues that have become important are hardly mentioned, for example, environmental issues and the role of women.

Moral theologians such as Fr Enda McDonagh recognise the achievement of GS but have noted other limitations.

• GS speaks from a European and First World perspective. *America* Its awareness of other 'worlds' and their problems is mainly restricted to the sections on economics and politics.

• The world's problems are seen as soluble in terms of co-operation, goodwill and the grace of God. This is because one of the strengths of the document is that it is characterised by a strong atmosphere of hope. The dark side of life and of theology is neglected, so that evil, suffering and the cross are rarely mentioned. The Church had so stressed these in the recent past that the pendulum now swung the other way. Indeed, GS looks so positively at the modern world that it could be accused of superficial optimism. In this regard, it was perhaps typical of the 1960s.

• The relationship between the world, the Church and the Kingdom is presented in a rather confused way. GS describes the work of God in the world, which is a major step forward, but it does not move on to show how this relates to the work of God in the Church.

WHAT CAME NEXT?

The most striking consequence which can be attributed to GS is the great movement for justice and peace which has become an integral part of Catholic life throughout the world from the local parish to the international level. This has manifested itself in many and diverse ways.

• The development of the 'theology of liberation' in Latin America was inspired not only by the social teaching in part two of GS but also by the whole approach to theology of part one. Taking the needs of ordinary people, that is, the deprived and marginalised, as the starting point for theology has led to new perspectives in Latin America which had an impact throughout the world. This is seen in 'black theology', 'Asian theology', and also in attempts to create a type of 'liberation theology' for Britain.

• Bishops throughout the world have pursued the concerns of GS vigorously. For example, the bishops of the USA have engaged in a process of discernment about their country's nuclear weapons and about its economic wealth.
The statements published as part of this process have had repercussions in the Church and society. The same is true of the great meetings of Latin American bishops held in Medellin (1968) and Puebla (1979), where the bishops examined their own situation in the light of the Council.

• Papal teaching has also been deeply influenced by GS. Pope Paul VI's two best known encyclicals draw on it: *The Progress of Peoples* (1967) and *On Human Life* (1968). Pope John Paul II refers to it for his theology of the human person and often refers to section 22: 'Christ reveals humanity to itself'. His encyclical *On Human Work* (1981) is a good example of developing GS's understanding of both culture and economics in an original approach to work, one of the great issues of today.

questions on the document

1. What things do you notice people doing to make this a better world?

2. 'GS has been called the most important document of the Council.' Why do you think some readers regard it so highly?

What do you think of the document?

What do you think is the single most important insight in part 1?

Which of the five areas in part 2 do you find most significant, and why?

If you are working in a group, take time:

TO SEE where we came from

TO UNDERSTAND the Pastoral Constitution

TO SHARE insights and responses

DISCUSS a possible way forward: where might we go from here?

MAKE a practical proposal or plan for the future.

Decree on the Mass Media (*Inter mirifica* – IM)

what is 'the mass media'?

Vatican II welcomed the inventions of modern technology, specifying the press, cinema, radio and television.

These are recognised as offering fresh ways of communicating news and ideas.

INTRODUCTION AND BACKGROUND

Widely regarded as the most lightweight document of Vatican II, IM is nevertheless the first document of an ecumenical council to address the means of social communication, 'the marvellous inventions of modern technology' which are such a distinctive feature of the twentieth-century world. Specified as outstanding among these are 'the press, the cinema, radio, television and such like' (1).

In its day-to-day operation, Vatican II was very conscious of the importance of the media which provided world-wide coverage of its debates and documentation. Press centres were set up in each of the main languages of the Council delegates to brief journalists on events and issues.

IM was voted through at the end of the second session without much discussion. In hindsight, it seems obvious that its concerns really belong with the topics discussed in the *Pastoral Constitution on the Church in the World of Today*. It would have made sense to have incorporated the Decree into GS as one chapter among others in part 2, but the importance of GS did not become apparent until the Council matured.

Given the importance of the mass media, Vatican II saw the need to address the 'main problems' associated with it.

Chapter 1:

IM says that the Church's mission to proclaim the Gospel involves knowledge and use of the media, especially by lay Christians. This involves the application of moral principles. Three problems are specified: the truthful communication of 'news' (5); the principles of moral standards which affect the arts (6); the care needed when 'moral evil' is being reported and described (7).

The use of the mass media raises important questions for the education of conscience, especially for young people who can be easily harmed or misled. Civil authorities are called to be vigilant about public morality (12).

Chapter 2:

IM encourages all members of the Church, pastors and lay Christians, to make good use of the media. It encourages a respectable Catholic press, wholesome films, radio and television programmes, and plays. These cannot be achieved without good training. Further concern is expressed about the moral development of young people (16).

Technical problems and the enormous costs of social communication are acknowledged. The Decree asks groups and individuals to be generous (17).

Each diocese is invited to organise an annual day to instruct the faithful to use the mass media responsibly. National and international centres are to be set up to foster Catholic activities in this field. A more detailed pastoral instruction will be published by the Holy See with the help of international experts (23).

Summary

9

STRENGTHS

The document offers an elementary introduction to the topic of social communications. IM's real achievement was to provide a basis for further development after the Council, in the light of issues introduced by GS.

LIMITATIONS

Prior to Vatican II, the Church had been slow, even reluctant to examine seriously new problems raised by modern society, including its own mission to communicate the good news to the modern world. As a document, IM lacked preparation. Given the importance of the subject, its treatment was moralistically narrow, negative in emphasis and lacking in theological depth. The importance of social communication in the Church's mission to the modern world was under-estimated by the Council. International experts were not invited to contribute to IM.

WHAT CAME NEXT?

A much more mature follow-up document was published by the Vatican in January 1971. See *Pastoral Instruction on the Means of Social Communication* in *Vatican Council II: More Postconciliar Documents*, ed. A. Flannery OP (1982).

A more complete document than IM, this was promised by IM23, which looked to the assistance of international experts, who had not been invited to contribute to the earlier document.

Catholic radio and television centres were established in several countries during the years after Vatican II, including the National Catholic Radio and Television Centre at Hatch End, Middlesex. A Centre for the Study of Communications and Culture was established in London in 1977.

Further work remains to be undertaken, including media education and explorations of the scope of the mass media for evangelisation and catechesis.

Declaration on Religious Freedom (*Dignitatis humanae* – DH)

INTRODUCTION

Although DH was subsequently seen by Pope Paul VI as one of the major texts of the Council, it was not easy to write. In fact, it proved to be Vatican II's most controversial document, its most bitterly disputed text. The great champions of DH were the North American Jesuit, John Courtney Murray, and Cardinal Bea of the Secretariat for Christian Unity. DH was not approved until the very end of the Council - after six drafts, opposition from a determined minority, much emotional debate, and over two thousand amendments.

General world interest in the debate and declaration was great. DH is addressed to 'all men and women of good will'. In this it is like Pope John XXIII's last encyclical letter, *Peace on Earth* (1963). The declaration concentrates on clarifying the place of religious freedom in every form of civil society and therefore in condemning all coercion.

BACKGROUND

Religious freedom has meant different things at different times, according to the type of society and culture in which the Church has existed. In some eras, the Church said that error had no rights; this explains why some who disagreed with the Church were persecuted.

In the early years of this century, some Catholics supported nazism and fascism in the belief that communism should be eradicated at all costs. In certain countries, such Catholics sought an authoritarian Church in partnership with an authoritarian state; they believed that liberty would undermine both Church and State.

DH firmly repudiates these ideas and embraces contemporary attitudes to freedom, attitudes also affirmed in GS17 (*The excellence of freedom*). Now the vision is of a free Church in a free society.

what is meant by 'religious freedom'?

The Council describes religious freedom as the right of persons and communities to social and civil liberty in religious matters.

Summary 9

Jesus answered...'For this I was born, and for this I came into the world, to testify to the truth. Everyone who belongs to the truth listens to my voice.' Pilate asked him, 'What is truth?'.

John 18: 37-38

How far?

The Declaration is in three parts.

1. An introduction on the rights of persons and communities to social and religious liberty in religious matters

People are increasingly aware of the dignity of the human person, responsible for personal judgment and freedom of conscience, not subject to external pressure or coercion.

God is made known to people through Christ and the Church. 'All people are bound to seek for the truth, especially about God and his Church, and when they have found it to embrace and keep it'.

In its treatment of religious freedom, the Council seeks to develop papal teaching 'on the inviolable rights of the human person and on the regulating of society by law'.

2. A presentation of the general principle of religious freedom

By virtue of being human, persons have a right to religious freedom and should never be subject to coercion by individuals or by society. This is a God-given right: to seek truth 'by free enquiry assisted by teaching... and by exchange and discussion in which people explain to each other the truth as they have discovered it or as they see it, so as to assist each other in their search' (3).

People must never be forced by the state to act against their conscience in private or public. This principle applies to individuals and to communities, in view of the social nature of humanity. It applies to religious communities and to families, to all citizens and social groups, who should be free from discrimination and force or fear.

Paragraph 8 states: 'People today are restricted in various ways and are in danger of being robbed of their power of free decision. At the same time many appear so assertive that in the name of freedom they reject all control and discount every duty of obedience'.

Therefore the Council 'exhorts all, and particularly those who have the charge of educating others, to apply themselves to bringing up people who will respect the moral law, obey legitimate authority and have a love for genuine freedom; that is, people who will use their own judgment to make decisions in the light of truth, plan their activities with a sense of responsibility, and freely combine their efforts with others to achieve all that is just and true'.

3. A consideration of religious freedom in the light of revelation

Vatican II's teaching about human rights is based not only on the dignity of the person but on divine revelation, made known by Jesus Christ, who respected people's freedom. 'One of the chief Catholic teachings, found in the word of God and repeatedly preached by the fathers of the Church, is that the response of people to God in faith should be voluntary; so no one must be forced to embrace the faith against his or her will. Indeed, the act of faith is by its very nature voluntary' (10).

God calls people to serve him by personal decision and not by external force. This is made clear by Jesus who attracted and invited followers rather than compelling them. 'For his kingdom is not upheld by the sword, but is founded on hearing and witnessing to the truth, and grows by the love whereby Christ raised on the cross draws people to himself' (11).

The apostles followed their master's example; so must the Church, although it has not always done so. The Church claims freedom of action in today's world, for it is the teacher of truth. It must never try to do this by going against the spirit of the Gospel. Religious freedom is recognised as a civil right by many states, but not by all. It needs adequate legal protection throughout the world.

We are putting no obstacles in anyone's way, so that no fault may be found with our ministry, but as servants of God we have commended ourselves in every way: through great endurance, in afflictions, hardships, calamities, beatings, imprisonments, riots, labours, sleepless nights, hunger; by purity, knowledge, patience, kindness, holiness of spirit, genuine love, truthful speech, and the power of God; with the weapons of righteousness for the right hand and for the left;

1 Corinthians 6:3-7

questions on the document

1. 'Error has no rights'. Why was this often said?

Why did Vatican II seek to change this idea and in what way?

2. Why is the Declaration on Religious Freedom important?

3. Is it right to force people to go to Mass?

If you are working in a group, take time:

TO SEE where we came from

TO UNDERSTAND the Declaration

TO SHARE insights and responses

DISCUSS a possible way forward: where might we go from here?

MAKE a practical proposal or plan for the future.

STRENGTHS

DH represented a dramatic change in Catholic attitudes, and several bishops found this new vision hard to accept. The bishops of the USA, with their traditions of democracy and the background of separation of Church and State, helped other bishops to accept the new approach. This explains why the debate about DH was so heated. The clear recognition that religious freedom belongs to everybody by reason of their human dignity was a new and forceful statement, as was the unambiguous condemnation of forms of discrimination. The demands of religious liberty have to be set against the need for public order, and paragraph 7 sought to do this.

LIMITATIONS

The declaration has been criticised for not giving sufficient attention to the danger of psychological coercion in the propaganda fed to modern society by the mass media.

Another important question which has been raised concerns attitudes to freedom within the Church. In the twentieth century, authority within the Church itself has frequently exercised reactionary control over its members, e.g. using the index of forbidden books and the *imprimatur*. During the years after Vatican II, most of these restrictions were lifted, as a more open and critical spirit spread within the Church.

WHAT CAME NEXT?

The question of freedom within the Church is still a source of tension, especially as national churches and certain theologians have sought greater freedom from Roman control. Since 1989, the collapse of communism in Eastern Europe has led to a remarkable increase in religious freedom in many countries, but also to a revival of ancient problems created by national rivalries and to new problems caused by selfish individualism and materialistic consumerism.

Declaration on the Church's Relation to non-Christian Religions

(*Nostra aetate* – NA)

[handwritten: 1) Not in original agenda 2) Original intent of doc – conflicts – the results 3) Dialogue ← what does healthy dialogue look like?]

INTRODUCTION

This topic was not on the original agenda of the Council. *[handwritten: like?]* The origin of this particular document lies in Pope John's concern about Jewish-Christian relations. The Holocaust, the extermination of six million Jews in Europe during the Second World War, is one of the great horrors of history. *[handwritten: But then extended to include other non Christian religions]*

BACKGROUND

The attitude of Christians to other religions has in general been very negative and fear-laden, though there have been notable exceptions, such as Matteo Ricci's dialogue with Chinese religion in the sixteenth century or Charles de Foucauld's love for Muslims in the nineteenth.

Cardinal Bea in a speech to the Council admitted that anti-Jewish ideas among Christians had helped Nazism to flourish. Pope John wished to ensure that Christian faith could never again be used to justify anti-semitism. To this end, he had asked that a special section be added to UR on relations with Jews.

This proved problematic because Jews themselves would not appreciate being treated as if they were another Christian Church and because Arabs saw any statement dealing solely with Jews as biased against them. So it was decided to develop a separate document on other religions, the first time a Council had ever addressed this issue.

The difficulty was to deal with religious sensitivities without being political. Ten per cent of Arabs are Christian, so Arab bishops at the Council were particularly sensitive to the issue of the State of Israel (rather than the People of Israel). Some feared the statement would support the State of Israel, so the text was revised to ensure that it could not be read in that way. The final text allayed such fears by placing the issue within the context of religious dialogue.

why does the council have a declaration to non-christian religions?

The great religious faiths of the world are becoming better known to one another. The Council specifically mentions four: Islam, Hinduism, Buddhism and Judaism.

'In our age, when the human race is being daily brought closer together and contacts between the various nations is more frequent, the Church is giving close attention to what is its relation to non-Christian religions' (1).

Summary

All people ask fundamental questions about life and share awareness of the holy mystery beyond this life. This expresses itself in various forms of religious practice and in the development of concepts which seek to explain these questions. Hinduism and Buddhism (and other religions) are commended as ways of liberation and illumination.

Without ceasing to preach Christ as the way, the truth and the life, the Church 'rejects nothing of those things which are true and holy in these religions' (2).

The Church respects especially those who worship the one true God, the creator of heaven and earth, namely Jews and Muslims. Muslims not only share this faith but also venerate Jesus as a prophet and honour his virgin mother Mary. In spite of a sad history of poor relations, Christians and Muslims should foster mutual understanding.

Above all, the document recommends a deep reflection on the relationship between Jews and Christians. The Church recognises that the followers of Christ are spiritually united with the descendants of Abraham, for not only Mary and hence Christ but also the first apostles were all Jews.

Although the Jewish leaders at the time of Christ pressed for his death, this does not mean that the Jews are rejected or accursed. They are still dear to God. 'The Church deplores feelings of hatred, persecutions and demonstrations of anti-semitism directed against the Jews at whatever time and by whomever.' (4).

All this is from God, who reconciled us to himself through Christ, and has given us the ministry of reconciliation.

2 Corinthians 5:18

STRENGTHS

The very existence of this document marks a dramatic leap forward in the Church's understanding of itself and the world. The Council had begun with the agenda of dialogue with other Christians; but to move to dialogue with other religions was an even bigger step. The condemnation of anti-semitism was a most important element in this dialogue. NA undoubtedly represents the first step on a long journey.

LIMITATIONS

The difficulty is that the document takes this first step without providing many hints about where it might go from here; there is no theology or guidelines for inter-religious dialogue.

The encouragement to develop Jewish-Christian dialogue is an important move towards a new awareness of Christian indebtedness to its roots and heritage in Judaism. The lack of any explicit call to repentance for the Holocaust is, however, a striking omission. Nevertheless, the clear condemnation of anti-semitism will always remain a landmark.

WHAT CAME NEXT?

There have been significant developments in Jewish-Christian relations. Councils for Christians and Jews have been set up in most countries. Much has been done to reduce the anti-semitic assumptions of Christian bible study and preaching, although anti-semitic comments about the inadequacy of the Old Testament and the malice of the Jews are still to be heard.

Misunderstandings are still common, for example, over the convent at Oswiencin (the site of atrocities at Auschwitz) but efforts at dialogue continue, symbolised by the visit of Pope John Paul to the synagogue of Rome in 1986, the first ever visit of a Pope to a synagogue. In 1994 the Vatican established full diplomatic relations with the State of Israel.

There have been world-wide developments in the field of inter-religious dialogue over the last thirty years; NA has enabled Catholics to take a full part in these. The movement of peoples amounting to mass migrations round the world, has brought greater local awareness and understanding among different cultures.

questions on the document

1. Which of the Hebrew Scriptures (Old Testament) are important to Christians, and why?

2. The Declaration seeks to redress injustices done to the Jews. Why and how?

3. The Council teaches Catholics to know about and to respect the beliefs of those who belong to the other great religions of the world. What would you say to your fellow Christians who think that to teach young Catholics about other faiths might be dangerous?

If you are working in a group, take time:

TO SEE where we came from

TO UNDERSTAND the Declaration

TO SHARE insights and responses

DISCUSS a possible way forward: where might we go from here?

MAKE a practical proposal or plan for the future.

At the level of monastic life, there has been a growing recognition of the monastic tradition as something shared in many religions. Much is being learned from Eastern religions about prayer and meditation.

At the global level, there have been international meetings of leaders such as that attended by the Pope in Assisi in 1987. Leaders of many different religions are finding that they share two convictions: the need to cherish creation and to work for peace.

Focus on Education for Christian Living

In one sense, this fourth section of our study of the Council documents offers a summary of only one document; Vatican II's Declaration on Christian Education (Gravissimum educationis).

However, importantly, it will consider in some detail examples from other major Council documents to illustrate the importance attached by the Council to Adult education in the renewal of the Church.

The authors of this book regard this as one of the most distinctive features of the teaching of the Second Vatican Council.

why focus on education?

Through education, people are introduced to culture, to the skills needed to survive, and to discovering and developing their unique personal identity.

questions on the document

1. Do you think Catholic schools are important today? Why or why not?

2. What are the characteristics of a good Catholic school?

3. How might Catholic schools contribute to 'life-long' Christian Education?

If you are working in a group, take time:

TO SEE where we came from

TO UNDERSTAND the Declaration

TO SHARE insights and responses

DISCUSS a possible way forward: where might we go from here?

MAKE a practical proposal or plan for the future.

Declaration on Christian Education

(*Gravissiumum educationis* – GE)

INTRODUCTION AND BACKGROUND

The background to GE is the rich and developing history of Catholic education, the way in which the Church has fulfilled the command of Jesus Christ to make disciples in every nation (Matthew 28, 18f). Historical accounts may be consulted in Catholic encyclopedias, noting the catechumenate in the early Christian centuries, the immense contribution of religious orders, the Church's role in fostering primary, secondary and tertiary education, the development of popular education since the 19th century, philosophies and psychologies of education, the flourishing modern catechetical movement, and the growth of interest in adult education.

SUMMARY (See pp. 125-126)

STRENGTHS AND LIMITATIONS

GE develops the principles stated in Pope Pius XI's 1929 encyclical letter on education (*Divini Illius Magistri*), by insisting on the Church's responsibility for temporal and spiritual education. Although not a particularly original or inspiring document, and limited to a view of education which affects young people, it is concerned to spell out a holistic Catholic view of basic educational principles, especially as these affect schools. A more detailed picture of Catholic education was to be developed in several documents written after Vatican II.

WHAT CAME NEXT?

This is developed in detail in *Education on other Council documents* and in the sections which follow:
What Came Next? – Universal Church (pp.134-135) and
What Came Next? – England and Wales (pp. 136-137).

Although GE is concerned primarily with the education of children and adolescents, its introductory paragraph mentions the continuing education of adults in modern society. While the declaration notes the increasing number of schools and other educational institutions, it regrets that many young people still lack a suitable education. GE aims to announce basic principles of Christian education, applied especially to schools, looking to further development of these after the Council to suit different regions.

Education is a basic right of all people in view of their human dignity, their eternal destiny, and their place in society. If true education is concerned to help people develop their physical, moral, intellectual and social gifts (1), all Christians have a right to a Christian education to help them develop into mature Christian adults. They benefit individually, but so does the whole Church, the body of Christ.

Parents are obliged to educate their children: they are indeed the 'primary and principal educators' of children, and 'the family is the first school of the social virtues which all societies need' (3).

GE emphasises the essential role of Christian families in promoting the life and development of the people of God. Civil society is asked to safeguard this right of parents and to provide additional educational resources, while the Church is 'bound to offer her children that sort of education by which their whole lives may be imbued with the spirit of Christ' (3).

Catechetical instruction strengthens Christian faith and life. Catholic schools occupy an important place in Church and society. Teachers have a noble and important vocation, which calls for special gifts of mind and heart, and 'a continual readiness for renovation and adaptation' (5).

Parents must be free to choose schools for their children. The state must protect this right and must therefore exclude any monopoly of schools. Parent associations are urged to contribute to the work of schools, especially to moral education. The Church's concern for the education of all its children includes the many children in non-Catholic schools and all who teach them.

A central paragraph (8) describes the characteristics of the Catholic school: a community animated by the gospel spirit

...to be renewed in the spirit of your minds, and to clothe yourselves in the new self, created according to the likeness of God in true righteousness and holiness.
Ephesians 4: 23-24

of freedom and love, concerned to promote an integral personal and spiritual education which illuminates knowledge by faith and prepares its pupils to be apostles in society.

Because teachers have 'the greatest possible influence in enabling a Catholic school to achieve its purposes' (8), they need to be trained, not only professionally but spiritually, to 'bear witness by their life and teaching to the one teacher Christ'. Their ministry involves working in partnership with parents and providing advice and friendship for young people.

The Church regards with great affection non-Catholic pupils in Catholic schools, especially in places where the Church is newly established. Different styles of educational establishments are distinguished.

Church communities are asked to make sacrifices to help Catholic schools, 'especially in caring for the needs of those who are poor in temporal goods, or are deprived of the help and affection of a family, or are strangers to the gift of faith' (9).

Paragraph 10 underlines the Church's concern to promote higher education and Catholic universities. In the latter, institutes of theology are to be established. Catholic higher education should be concerned with the spiritual formation of students, and also with promoting ecumenical dialogue and deeper research. Cooperation at diocesan, national and international levels is encouraged.

The declaration ends with a word of thanks and encouragement for all involved in education. They help not only to renew the Church but to improve its effective presence in the world.

Education in other Council documents

The Council gives a strong emphasis to the need for education in all parts of the Church today. The rest of this section gives the teaching as found in various documents. The documents are grouped as they have been presented in this book.

FOCUS ON SPIRITUALITY

The Constitutions on the Sacred Liturgy and on Divine Revelation emphasise the importance of intelligible worship helping Christians to grow in faith, which is their personal response to God's revelation. Meeting God in prayer and in community influences the lives of believers.

In Vatican II's understanding of liturgy, 'the church wants all believers to take a full, conscious and active part in liturgical celebration' (SC14), and this cannot be achieved without 'appropriate formation'. That is why SC18 asked those responsible for pastoral care to foster active participation by people in the liturgy, 'both inwardly and outwardly, in ways suited to their age, the circumstances they are in, the kind of life they lead, and their level of religious culture'. In the course of the liturgical year, homilies will explain 'the hidden realities of faith and the guiding principles of Christian life' (SC52).

DV8 emphasises that the expression 'what has been handed down from the apostles' includes everything that helps the people of God to live a holy life and to grow in faith'. This is a work of education. Preaching is to be 'nourished and ruled by holy scripture' (DV21) so that the Father can come lovingly to meet his children and talk with them. Easy access to holy scripture should be available to all the Christian faithful (DV22) to nourish and revitalise their faith. Just as faithful and frequent reception of the eucharistic mystery makes the Church's life grow, so we may hope that its spiritual life will receive a new impulse from increased devotion to the word of God, which 'abides for ever' (DV26).

FOCUS ON THE CHURCH

Vatican II's teaching about the Church emphasises the active participation of all Christians in the renewal of the Church's life and mission. For this they need to be educated.

'All the faithful of every state and condition are called by the Lord, each in their own way, to that perfect holiness whereby the Father is perfect' (LG11). The lives of the faithful are enriched by the gifts of the Holy Spirit (LG12) for the renewal and building up of the Church. One sign of this is the presence of catechumens, who are embraced by Mother Church as her own (LG14). 'By preaching the gospel, the Church draws its hearers to faith and the profession of faith' (LG17), so that they may grow to Christian maturity.

LAITY

In examining the vocation of lay Christians, Vatican II insists that people, 'while carrying out their responsibilities in the world in the ordinary conditions of life, do not allow any separation of their union with Christ from their daily lives, but rather grow in this union by doing their work according to God's will' (AA4). The apostolate of lay Catholics and the pastoral ministry complement each other and are expressed in witness and word (AA6). Examples are listed in AA10's description of parish life and in the decree's commentary on the apostolate of various types of lay people.

It is hardly necessary to underline that 'the apostolate can only attain its full effectiveness through an integrated and many-sided formation', which fosters 'all truly human values...especially the art of living and working together in fellowship and of talking together', for instance using Cardijn's educational method of seeing, judging and acting in all things in the light of faith, 'so as to form and perfect themselves, with others, and so enter into effective service of the Church' (AA29). The development of resources and centres for the lay apostolate is noted in AA32.

BISHOPS

'Among the principal tasks of bishops the preaching of the Gospel is pre-eminent' (LG25). All pastors are called 'to acknowledge and promote the dignity and responsibility of the laity in the Church' (LG37), so that 'the whole Church, strengthened by all its members, is able more effectively to carry out its mission for the life of the world'. All members of the people of God are called to an active role in evangelisation and catechesis: to 'make manifest to all, even as they carry out their work here on earth, that love with which God has loved the world' (LG41).

CD12 emphasises that, in discharging their obligation to teach, bishops should proclaim to humanity the Gospel of Christ: 'With the courage imparted by the Spirit, they should call people to faith or strengthen them in living faith'. The teaching role of bishops is not confined to specifically religious matters: 'they should propose methods for finding an answer to questions of the utmost gravity: the ownership, increase, and just distribution of material wealth; peace and war; the effective fellowship of all peoples. They should present Christian doctrine in ways relevant to the needs of the times. Obviously, such teaching should deal with the most pressing difficulties and problems which weigh people down... They should make evident the maternal solicitude of the Church for everyone whether they are believers or not, and take particular care to further the interests of the poor and the underprivileged to whom the Lord has sent them to preach the Gospel' (PO13).

Further paragraphs of CD develop a fuller pastoral picture of the bishop's teaching responsibilities: 'to make people's faith, enlightened by doctrine, a living faith, explicit and active'... This means that the catechists who collaborate with the bishops 'should have an ample knowledge of the teaching of the Church as well as theoretical knowledge and practical experience of the principles of psychology and the methodology of pedagogy' (CD14). The role of catechists is vitally important, especially in communities without a resident pastor.

PRIESTS

In discussing the ministry of priests, PO emphasises the key role of priests as the fellow-workers of the bishops having 'as their first charge to announce the gospel of God to all', arousing faith in the heart of non-believers and strengthening it in the heart of believers: 'If in their preaching priests are really to reach the minds of their audience, which is often very difficult in modern conditions, then they must not merely expound God's message in a

general and abstract way, but apply the enduring truth of the Gospel to the concrete situations of life' (PO4).

'It is for priests, as educators in the faith, to see either personally or through others that every one of the faithful is led by the Holy Spirit to develop their own vocation in the light of the Gospel, with a love that is personal and active, and with the freedom wherewith Christ has set us free. Of little use are ceremonies, however beautiful, or societies, however flourishing, if they are not geared to producing Christian maturity' (PO6).

Necessarily, 'the task of the pastor is not limited to the care of the faithful as individuals, but also properly extends to the formation of real community' - a community with a true sense of responsibility for mission, while not neglecting concern for the welfare of all its members, notably 'the recently baptised, who need to be led by stages to understand and to lead the Christian life' (PO6). The task involves priests confidently entrusting responsibilities to the laity in the service of the Church, 'giving them freedom for action, and indeed inviting them when appropriate to take up works on their own initiative' (PO9). This view of pastoral care involves approaching Catholics who have lapsed from the sacraments, as well as making contact with other Christians, and showing care for all who do not acknowledge Christ as their saviour.

In the same paragraph (PO10), lay Catholics are asked 'to share their priests' concerns and help them as they can with prayer and practical assistance, so that they may more easily overcome difficulties and fulfil their mission with greater fruitfulness'.

Appropriate supports for priests include pastoral courses and conferences, especially for newly appointed parish priests or those in a new situation (PO19). This is consistent with the teaching of OT, where 'spiritual formation should be closely combined with doctrinal and pastoral formation' (OT8), and where 'solid personal maturity' will be formed as future priests 'gradually learn to form their own discipline' so 'they may become accustomed to use freedom wisely and to act energetically on their own initiative and cooperate with colleagues and laity' (OT11).

Students for the priesthood are also to learn how to communicate eternal truths 'in a way that is suitable for their contemporaries' (OT16). 'In general, those gifts are to be developed in the students which most favour dialogue with people. Such are the capacity of listening to others, and of opening their hearts in a spirit of charity to the various circumstances of human need' (OT19).

ECUMENISM

Finally, in this second group of documents, it is worth pointing to the role of education in ecumenical work, including dialogue, where 'everyone gains a truer knowledge and more just appreciation of the teaching and life of each community', as they 'undertake with vigour the task of renewal and reform' (UR4).

The biblical and liturgical movements, the preaching of the word of God , catechetics, the apostolate of the laity, new forms of religious life, the spirituality of married life, the Church's social teaching and activity are all instanced as 'promises and guarantees for the future progress of ecumenism' (UR6). Study (to understand the outlook of other Christians) is encouraged (UR9), and also a renewal of theology, so that 'the Catholic faith may be explained more profoundly and precisely', with due regard for the 'hierarchy of truths' (UR11).

MISSIONARY ACTIVITY

As one would expect, the Council's description of the Church's missionary activity describes the work of the Holy Spirit in uniting the entire Church and furnishing it with different hierarchical and charismatic gifts (AG4); gifts which are to be used in the life and mission of the Church, especially in non-Christian societies where Christians are called to discover 'with joy and reverence... the seeds of the Word which lie hidden' (AG11). Christians discover these even as they love people 'with that same affection with which God has sought out humankind', especially the poor and afflicted, whose joys, sorrows and problems Christ's faithful share (AG12) - a view stated even more powerfully in GS 1.

AG amplifies SC's rediscovery of the catechumenate, stressing that Christian initiation is 'the work not only of catechists and priests but of the entire community of the faithful' (AG14). An essential aspect of the Church's missionary activity is forming the Christian community (AG 15-18), in which the ministry of catechists is 'of the highest importance' and in which 'congregations of the faithful, daily more aware of themselves, are to become living communities of faith, of liturgy and of charity', not to speak of justice and other signs of Christian maturity (AG19), including a zealous priesthood, committed to dedicated service of the community (AG39).

The new Rite of Initiation of Christian Adults (RCIA) promised by Vatican II, was published in 1974, and was gradually translated into various languages. It has been a source of inspiration and renewal in many communities.

FOCUS ON THE CHURCH IN THE WORLD OF TODAY

The increase of esteem for an educated adult laity is very apparent in GS and related documents, which link Christian maturity to human dignity and freedom. IM3 relates specifically the use of the media to Christian education, while DH3 insists that 'truth is to be sought in a manner benefitting the dignity and social nature of the human person, namely by free enquiry assisted by teaching and discussion in which people explain to each other the truth as they have discovered it or as they see it, so as to assist each other in their search'. People are encouraged 'to use their own judgment to make decisions in the light of truth, plan their activities with a sense of responsibility, and freely combine their efforts with others to achieve all that is just and true' (DH8). The God who 'calls people to serve him in spirit and in truth, so that they are bound to him by personal decision and not by external force... looks to the dignity of the human person, whom he has created and who needs to be guided by his own judgment and enjoy his freedom' (DH11).

Dynamic Approach

GS contains much that is relevant to Vatican II's understanding of adult education. It emphasises the duty to examine the signs of the times and to interpret them in the light of the Gospel, so Catholics can be aware of 'the world in which we live', as they struggle with 'continuing human questionings on the meaning of this life and the life to come and on how they are related' (GS4).

The movement from a more static view of things to one which is more dynamic and evolutionary gives rise to 'new combinations of problems which call for new analyses and syntheses' (GS5). Christian faith 'shows everything in a new light' (GS11), but it is assisted by the intellect (GS15).

Believers are warned that they are capable of 'concealing the true features of God and religion... through the neglect of education in the faith or false explanations of its doctrines or even through the faults in their religious, moral and social lives' (GS19). The witness of a 'living and mature' faith is the opposite of this (GS21), and it allows believers to 'hand on to posterity grounds for living and for hope' (GS31).

This involves recognising that the Church 'may not always have a ready answer to particular questions, wishing to combine the light of revelation with universal experience so that illumination can be forthcoming on the direction which humanity has recently begun to take' (GS33). It involves attending to 'the deepest hunger of the human heart', a spiritual hunger, a search for meaning, in which 'whoever follows Christ, the perfect human being, becomes more of a human being' (GS41).

Maturity

The implication is that though 'the laity may expect enlightenment and spiritual help from the clergy... they should not expect that their pastors always have the expertise needed to provide a concrete and ready answer to every problem which arises, even the most serious ones, for this is not their mission. The laity, as enlightened with Christian wisdom and paying careful attention to the magisterium, have their own part to play' (GS43).

The Church not only provides help but also receives help from the modern world, for its members are called to 'listen to the various voices of our day, discerning them and interpreting them', and evaluating them (GS44). In this world, 'a new humanism is being born in which the human is defined above all in terms of our responsibility to our brothers and sisters and to history' (GS55). This implies a healing of rifts which have often tended to separate faith and culture: 'In pastoral care not just theological principles but also the discoveries of the secular sciences, especially of psychology and sociology, should be recognised and applied so that the faithful may be brought to a more refined and more mature life of faith' (GS62).

why a new catechism?

(Extracts from *Guidelines*, Bishops' Conference of England and Wales, 1994)

The Synod of Bishops which met in 1985 was called together by the Pope to celebrate and re-affirm the message of the Second Vatican Council and to carry its work forward. The message which the Bishops issued at the end of the Synod said: "Today we feel impelled towards a deeper understanding of the true significance of Vatican Two, in order to respond to the world's new challenges and to those which Christ ever addresses to the world."

Prominent among the challenges identified by the Synod was the need to preach the Gospel to all peoples. The synod Fathers noted that this demands a new initiative in evangelisation and catechesis. In order to respond to this urgent challenge, the Bishops at the Synod asked for a Catechism or compendium of the whole of Catholic doctrine, of both faith and morals, which would be 'a point of reference' for catechetical materials produced in various regions.

In introducing the Catechism, the Commission which prepared it emphasised that the Catechism is dedicated to the full and faithful expression and implementation of the teaching of the Second Vatican Council. Pope John Paul echoed this in Fidei Depositum, *when he wrote that the Catechism will 'make a very important contribution to that work of renewing the whole life of the church, as desired and begun by the Second Vatican Council'.*

WHAT CAME NEXT? – UNIVERSAL CHURCH

Schools

• Important post-conciliar documents expanded and updated aspects of the thought of GE in relation to Catholic schools, in view of further changes in Church and society. The Roman Congregation for Catholic Education published three documents:
Catholic Schools, 1977;
Lay Catholics in Schools: Witnesses to Faith, 1982;
The Religious Dimension of Education in a Catholic School, 1988.

Catechesis

• Post-conciliar Vatican documents which affect catechesis (the activity which leads the community and individuals to maturity of faith) are:
The General Catechetical Directory, 1971;
The Rite of Christian Initiation of Adults (RCIA), 1974;
Pope John Paul II's letter on *Catechesis in Our Time;* (1979);
Adult Catechesis in the Christian Community: some principles and guidelines (a report of the International Council for Catechesis, 1990).
In 1992, the *Catechism of the Catholic Church*, was completed. The first English version was published in 1994.

The General Catechetical Directory was prepared by the Sacred Congregation for the Clergy, which consulted international catechetical experts. Divided into six parts, the Directory sets out to study the problem of teaching the faith to contemporary men and women in a rapidly changing society.

Using GS and DV, it describes the contemporary world and Church as the context for catechesis and evangelisation. The Directory considers the content of the Christian message, its most important elements, and the way it needs to be adjusted to the age and situation of the people to whom it is being presented. It also discusses the formation and resources needed by catechists, and the place of catechesis in the overall pastoral work of the Church.

The document on *Adult Catechesis in the Christian Community* is a presentation in 86 paragraphs of the most significant aspects of this subject. 'It touches on common issues, problems and solutions, which seem prevalent throughout the world, fully recognising that inculturation will have to be made in the local churches'. The document studies the adults to whom catechesis is directed; points of reference for adult catechesis; and guidelines for practical implementation.

The *Catechism of the Catholic Church* was produced by an international commission of cardinals and bishops (as a result of wide consultation) in response to a decision of the 1985 Synod of Bishops. The Catechism offers a comprehensive account of the foundations and content of Catholic doctrine, covering both faith and morals, in the light of the Second Vatican Council and the whole of the Church's tradition. A book of 700 pages, aimed principally at bishops and those who share in their teaching ministry, it covers four main areas:

what Catholics believe;
how they celebrate faith in liturgy and sacraments;
how they can live a morally faithful life;
how and why they pray.

Growth of interest in adult education

• CD14, in discussing the teaching office of bishops, had noted that bishops were to ensure that catechetical instruction was to be 'given with zealous care to children, adolescents, young people and even adults'. By the time the *General Catechetical Directory* was published (only six years later), the catechesis of adults was presented as 'the principal kind of catechesis, towards which all other forms, while always needed, are directed'.

What is the explanation of the extraordinary growth in conviction about adult catechesis in the Church during the years following Vatican II? Explanation lies in the teaching of the Council itself, and in the eventual realisation that the whole Church needed to be educated as the bishops had been during the Council.

a point of reference

(Extracts from the *Guidelines*, Bishops' Conference of England and Wales, 1994)

The Catechism is intended to be 'a point of reference' for local catechetical texts, including catechisms. This clear purpose is stated in the Prologue of the Catechism (11). It underlines the importance of the work to be done locally in order to adapt the text and use it fruitfully in our own circumstances. The Prologue also stresses the necessity of adaptation:

Given the purpose of this work, the adaptation of doctrinal presentations and catechetical methods cannot be carried out here. Such indispensable adaptation, required by the differences of culture, age, spiritual life, and social and ecclesial condition among the People of God, belongs in other catechisms following on this work, and is the particular task of those who teach the faith (24)

Those who teach or catechise will carry out this adaptation by developing texts drawing upon the Catechism and suitable in method and approach for particular groups of people or contexts. They will also be able to use the Catechism as a source to deepen their own understanding and enrich their teaching. It is not meant to make any existing catechetical texts redundant but it will serve as a resource for their continuing use and for the new materials we will need to develop.

WHAT CAME NEXT? – ENGLAND AND WALES

In the area of catechetics and religious education, the years of theological ferment which followed Vatican II were marked by several controversial experiments. In England and Wales, many of these were associated with Corpus Christi College, London (1965-75), an institute for the training of catechists. Other disputes were directed around RE methods and textbooks used in schools, especially secondary schools. A lively debate continues, since it is still unresolved.

Education and Formation

Although Bishop B.C. Butler's book *The Theology of Vatican II* (*DLT*, 1967, revised ed. 1981), saw one of the great failings of the post-conciliar years to be the lack of adult education, many parts of the Church at least began to direct new energy into adult education. As far as the English and Welsh Church is concerned, several references have already been made to the National Pastoral Congress (1980), which amounted to a formal reception of the teaching of Vatican II.

One of the seven sectors of the Congress focused on Christian Education and Formation, but a reading through the Congress reports, resolutions and the bishops' response called *The Easter People* shows the unmistakeable emphasis which all delegates attached to adult education and formation. For instance, one resolution stated: 'In view of the fact that the teachings of the Second Vatican Council are not being sufficiently implemented, urgent consideration and provision should be given to a deeper formation of priests and people, so that they may work together in the spirit of the Gospel'.

One of the notable effects which followed the Congress was the enthusiastic introduction into the life of many parishes of the new Rite of Christian Initiation of Adults (RCIA). The Congress's request for a national catechetical centre or pastoral institute never became a reality, since the Congress was never followed up nationally. On the other hand, diocesan catechetical teams and their various educational initiatives have flourished. Lack of space prevents a detailed account of these, and of the growing retreat movement which has promoted the spiritual development of the adult church.

Bishops' Initiatives

Since 1985, *Living and Sharing Our Faith*, a National Project of Catechesis and Religious Education initiated by the Bishops' Conference of England and Wales, has published several resources to help the religious education of the Catholic community in home, school and parish.

After the Education Reform Act of 1988, several initiatives were introduced to encourage the revitalisation of Catholic schools. A Coordinating Committee for Inservice, Evaluation and Appraisal in Catholic schools (CCIEA) prepared development materials which were published by the Bishops Conference of England and Wales. The National Catholic Education Council was re-organised into a new Catholic Education Service to coordinate the renewal process in Catholic schools in every diocese and to serve the educational needs of the Catholic community from the cradle to the grave. The Bishops' Conference Department of Catholic Education and Formation oversaw these developments, while individual bishops acted as spokesmen for the Catholic community, notably Cardinal Hume and Bishop David Konstant.

The need to respond to new developments in education and in the life of the Church will continue to call for new efforts. In 1994, the *Guidelines* issued by the Bishops' Conference at the time of the publication of the English translation of the *Catechism of the Catholic Church* drew attention, as does the Catechism itself, to the importance for local adaptation and development of catechetical resources (see *A Point of Reference* p.136). As such development continues, the Catechism can help catechists and teachers to find a good balance between sound content and appropriate methods to use in education and catechesis.

The results of all these initiatives may be uneven, but they represent a continuing series of small steps to implement the vision of John Henry Newman's challenge (as expressed in *The Present Position of Catholics in England*, lectures delivered in 1896) quoted in the report of the Liverpool Congress: **"We want a laity... who know their religion, who enter into it, who know just where they stand, who know what they hold and what they do not, who know their creed so well that they can give an account of it, who know so much history that they can defend it."**

questions on christian education in the documents

1. Why do the Council documents attach such importance to the education of the entire Catholic community?

2. How seriously does your local church take the continuing education of its adult members?

3. Traditionally, religious education was regarded as appropriate for children in school, but it is now considered to be a life-long task. How do you account for this change?

If you are working in a group, take time:

TO SEE where we came from

TO UNDERSTAND the Documents

TO SHARE insights and responses

DISCUSS a possible way forward: where might we go from here?

MAKE a practical proposal or plan for the future.

ANTI-SEMITISM

'Semitic' refers to the races supposedly descended from Shem, son of Noah (see Genesis 11). Anti-Semitism means anti-Jewish feeling, and it has been recognised as endemic in Europe since Roman times. In the twentieth century, it reached its most horrible expression in the Holocaust or 'Shoah', in which from five to six million Jews were exterminated as part of the racial cleansing policies of nazi Germany.

ASSUMPTION OF OUR LADY

One of the oldest and most celebrated feasts of the Blessed Virgin Mary. No mention of such an event is found in Scripture but the liturgical commemoration is among the oldest in the Church. It commemorates the taking into heaven of Mary, body and soul, at the end of her life on earth. The dogma of the Assumption of Mary was proclaimed as a truth of faith by Pope Pius XII in 1950.

ATHEISM

Denial of the existence of God or of any possibility of knowing God, or of allowing this knowledge to have any consequences in human life. GS (19-21) notes the various causes of atheism, including modern forms of theoretical atheism, and the attitude of the Christian Church to it.

BASIC CHRISTIAN COMMUNITY

A 'Basic Christian Community' (BCC) is a group of the faithful united within a parish or section of the local Church for study of the Bible and for the application of biblical values to social, political and economic life. 'Basic Communities witness to positive values wherever their members endeavour simply and sincerely to give form to the Gospel in their everyday lives.' (Pope John Paul II). There are more than 150,000 BCCs in Brazil alone, where they have flourished in response to the pastoral and evangelising need of the Church.

CATECHESIS/CATECHUMEN/CATECHUMENATE

Catechesis is the process by which Christian faith is nourished and educated. Sometimes it means passing on the essentials of the faith to new members, but in a wider sense it is co-extensive with Christian teaching from the first announcement of the Good News to the highest form of theology. It seeks to present the word of God as a living reality in the Christian community and since Vatican II emphasis has been placed on adult catechesis.

Catechumens are those preparing for reception into the Church. They receive instruction in different ways and in stages according to their needs during their time of preparation for the sacraments of initiation, which is called the catechumenate. According to LG 14, catechumens are already members of the Church, even before they are baptised.

CATECHISM

Originally the faith was passed on through oral witness and teaching derived from the liturgy. When the faith was passed on by parents, sponsors and other members of the Christian community, it often took on the character of questions and answers and was written into books. The Council of Trent sponsored a catechism which was the basis for local catechisms. The 1992 Catechism of the Catholic Church is a reference book for bishops and catechists, which presents Catholic teaching in the light of Vatican II. (English translation, 1994)

CATHOLIC

The Greek word from which 'catholic' is derived means 'universal' or 'wholeness'. Its first written use is in a letter from St Ignatius of Antioch to the Christians of Smyrna (c.107AD). To describe the Church as catholic means that it accepts the teaching of Christ as being open to all peoples in all nations and at all times: 'Go, make disciples of all nations.' (Matthew 28, 19). Catholicism was accepted from earliest times as one of the marks or distinguishing signs of the Church.

CATHOLIC ACTION

A movement in the twentieth-century Church, encouraged by Pope Pius XI and his immediate successors, through which lay-people are involved in the work of mission in their own culture and society. It refers to groups which under the direct authority of Church leaders take on works of charity and justice.

CHARISMS

These are gifts or graces bestowed by God for the good of the Church. An essential feature of the continuing life of the Christian community, they appear in constantly new forms and have to be rediscovered. See 1 Corinthians 12f. and LG 12.

'Charismatic movements' in the Church are characterised by personal enthusiasm in relation to Jesus as Lord and Saviour, by a strong emphasis on prayer, openness to the Holy Spirit and the sharing of spiritual gifts in community.

COLLABORATIVE MINISTRY

Collaborative ministry is a way of showing that all the gifts of the Holy Spirit are for the upbuilding of the Church, and that they are available to all Christians through baptism and Confirmation. Clergy and laity cooperate in using the gifts needed for the work of Christ in the world. Together they work according to various roles in response to the situation and to the gifts of each.

COLLEGIALITY

In relation to Church government, collegiality expresses the view that, collectively, the bishops of the Church, in union with the Pope, have supreme teaching and pastoral authority over the whole Church. Especially associated with Vatican II (see LG 22 and CD 3-4), collegiality calls attention to the proper relationship between communion and authority in the Church.

CRITICAL HISTORICAL METHODS

Various disciplines contribute to the understanding of sacred Scripture. They include biblical languages and translation, criticism of texts, the study of literary forms and genres, and awareness of cultural, geographical and historical influences on the sacred writers.

The Scriptures have been studied since ancient times, but in the nineteenth century investigation of 'historical' truth was popular with scholars, and Church authorities sometimes feared that the true meaning of the sacred Scriptures would be lost if they were treated like any other historical texts.

The 1902 Pontifical Biblical Commission was caught up in the modernist crisis, but studies which followed the encyclical *Divino Afflante Spiritu* (On Biblical Studies), 1943, helped to instigate a renewal of Scripture in the life of the Church, reflected in the Dogmatic Constitution on Divine Revelation. The Biblical Commission was re-established in 1969.

DIACONATE

This is the ministry of deacons, first mentioned in the New Testament (Acts 6, 1-6; Romans 16, 1-2). It may be a step which leads on to priestly ordination, but it is also a ministry in its own right, restored by Vatican II (see LG 29), and open to married men.

DIALOGUE

In the context of the Church, dialogue (conversation or communication) encourages discussion which recognises the right of each participant to be heard. Respect for and recognition of the presence of God's Spirit in the world, in many and various ways, encourages the Church to want to relate to all people and to dialogue with them all.

DIVINE OFFICE

The public prayer of the Church, for the praise of God. It is also called the 'liturgy of the hours' because it marks times of prayer throughout the day. It consists of psalms, Scripture readings and other prayers, contained in the Roman breviary. The two principal parts of the Office are Morning and Evening Prayer.

The Divine Office was reformed by Vatican II (see SC 83-101) and is recommended as a form of community prayer for all Christians. It is a sacred obligation for priests and for those in solemn vows.

DOCTRINE/DOGMA

Doctrine means 'teaching'. Vatican I defines dogma as the solemn teaching of the Church. It states that revealed truth may be set forth by the Church explicitly and definitely.

ECUMENISM/ECUMENICAL MOVEMENT

These words refer to the pursuit of unity or to the movement of Christians towards the unity willed by Christ (John 17). Divisions and schisms have been a scandal to the world, but in the twentieth century the ecumenical movement is a serious attempt to recognise this scandal and work towards the healing of divisions.

ECUMENICAL COUNCIL

A meeting of the bishops of the whole Church, called or ratified by the Pope. There have been only twenty-one Ecumenical Councils. (see p. 11).

ENCYCLICAL

A pastoral letter addressed by the Pope to the whole Church, which generally concerns matters of doctrine, morals or discipline.

ENLIGHTENMENT

The eighteenth century is called the age of Enlightenment or Reason, because of the predominance of rational and scientific attitudes in its leading thinkers, especially in their relationship with religion, ethics and natural law. Because it downgraded the significance of revealed religion, the Enlightenment was said to lead to subjectivism, secularism and excessive optimism regarding human perfectibility.

ESCHATOLOGY

The 'eschaton' (Greek) is the 'end-time', the end of life in this world. Christian teaching about eschatalogy includes the 'four last things' (death, judgment, heaven and hell) and points to the final state of God's creation at the end of time.

EVANGELISATION

In a broad sense, evangelisation means all missionary activity having as its goal the renewal of all creation according to God's purpose, including drawing people into relationship with Christ. In a more restricted sense, it refers to the stage of missionary catechesis, in which the basic Christian message is presented to prospective Christians. In many instances, evangelisation must be preceded by pre-evangelisation or a process of listening to the individual's needs and questions, in order to respond in a way that presents faith as a viable option.

See Pope Paul VI's Exhortation on Evangelisation (1975). *Evangelii Nuntiandi.*

EX CATHEDRA

'From the chair' (of St Peter). The phrase is used for the rare occasions when the Pope, guided by the revelation of Scripture and Tradition, makes an infallible pronouncement on matters of faith and morals to be held by the whole Church.

EXCOMMUNICATION

The exclusion of a baptised member from the communion of believers. It is a penalty for certain serious offences specified in Canon Law. Exclusion lasts until such time as the person excluded repents and receives absolution.

GRACE

Grace is a free gift of God, a mysterious participation in God's life. The word is understood to mean God's favour, in the sense of God's gratuitous love for human beings and angels, or a gift received in virtue of that love. All grace is mediated by Christ through the Holy Spirit, and the principal means of grace are the sacraments, prayer and good works.

GREGORIAN CHANT

Going back to the third century AD, this is a form of religious music called after Pope St Gregory the Great (540-606). It consists of prayerful settings of liturgical Latin texts. It is modal music, not based on major and minor keys, and is not metric but has a rhythm of its own, which is said to breathe the calm and serenity of eternity.

HEBREW BIBLE

A collection of books, originally written in Hebrew, known by Christians as the Old Testament. The Jewish people call these Scriptures 'Tanakh'. The use of the term 'Hebrew Bible' respects the dignity of the ancient Jewish Scriptures.

HERESY

The denial of some Christian truth by a baptised person who remains a nominal Christian. It involves resistance to the revelation of God who communicates through Scripture, Tradition and the teaching authority of the Church. Heresies have sometimes been significant as occasions for the clarification and development of doctrine.

IMPRIMATUR

From Latin: 'Let it be published'. It constitutes ecclesiastical permission to publish books of a religious character used as basic texts in institutes of learning, but was formerly used more widely in relation to books written by Catholics. It does not necessarily imply approval of the viewpoint or manner of handling the subject.

INCULTURATION

A modern term which refers to the relationship between the Gospel and culture. All human beings are affected by the culture in which they live. God is present in culture (see AG 11 on 'seeds of the word'), so the Church's mission of evangelisation requires an awareness of the values of human culture, so as to penetrate and elevate culture through the power of the Gospel.

INDEX

The 'index' was a list of published writings forbidden to Catholics as being dangerous to faith and morals. The index was abolished in 1966.

INFALLIBILITY

To be infallible is to be protected from making a mistake or being wrong. The doctrine of infallibility is based on the promise of Christ to be with his Church ' all days, even to the end of time' (Matthew 28, 20) and on the centuries-long tradition of the Church.

INTERCOMMUNION

The common celebration and reception of the Eucharist by members of different Christian churches. The Catholic Church permits intercommunion only in certain circumstances and on particular occasions.

LAITY

From 'laos' (Greek), meaning lay people as distinct from clerics in holy orders. "The laity are those of Christ's faithful, who have been incorporated into him by baptism and who live 'in the world'." (AG 15)

LIBERALISM

A movement and trend of thought in the nineteenth century, favouring liberty, independence and progress in moral, intellectual, social, economic and political life. Some types of liberalism were seen as harmful to Christianity because it was feared 'freedom of thought' would undermine the Church's authority; but liberalism may be patterned according to sound principles of Christian teaching, for instance, respect for human dignity.

LIBERATION THEOLOGY

A style of theology developed in Latin America after Vatican II to interpret the Christian message in practical application to the life and mission of people today. Its concern for human rights and aspirations in this world, not only in the next, represents an understanding of salvation as the coming of the Kingdom of God in time and not only in eternity. It would stress the role of the Church in the continuing mission of Christ who came to set people free.

LOCAL CHURCH

A group of Christians who meet regularly to celebrate Eucharist, for community, and to plan their corporate activities. Local Church is distinguished from the universal Church. In New Testament language, the term 'church' often means the local community of believers, coming together under the bishop, and this unit is called a diocese. When used theologically the Local Church is the Church fully present in a particular location. In a narrower sense, it can mean a congregation or parish. (See LG 26-27.

MODERNISM

Historically, this was a loose-knit movement at the beginning of the twentieth century, when scholars of different fields tried to bridge the gap between Christianity and the world of modern thought and knowledge. Their work was labelled 'modernism', was said to undermine the objective validity of religious belief and practices, and was condemned as 'the synthesis of all heresies' by Pope Pius X in the encyclical *Pascendi* (1907).

MYSTICAL BODY

An image or metaphor, used by St Paul, who portrays the Church as the 'mystical body' of Christ (1 Corinthians 12; Romans 12; Ephesians 1). All Christians are members of this body, through which Christ mediates his faith, hope and love to the world. (See *Christifideles laici*)

PASCHAL MYSTERY

The name given to the death, resurrection and ascension of Christ regarded as one single saving event. The Church celebrates this each year particularly during Holy Week and Easter, in the liturgy of each Sunday, and also through the whole pattern of its sacramental and liturgical life

PASTORAL

The adjective relates to 'pastor' or shepherd, and is linked with the ministry of Jesus as Good Shepherd. (See John 10: 11-18). Pastoral ministry is used to describe the care of people, since part of the Church's basic mission is to bring the Good News of Christ to all humanity. (See CD 2-3 and GS 3.)

POPE/ROMAN PONTIFF

The familiar name given to the Bishop of Rome as head of the Roman Catholic Church. The word means 'father'. The word 'pontiff' (from the Latin, pons - bridge) refers to the role of the Pope as a link or bridge between heaven and earth.

RCIA

Abbreviation for the Rite of Christian Initiation of Adults, promulgated by the Congregation for Divine Worship in 1972, in response to Vatican II's decision to restore the adult catechumenate. It marks different stages in the preparation of adults for the sacraments of initiation: baptism, confirmation and eucharist.

ROMAN CURIA

The officials of the central administration of the Church based in the Vatican City. Pope Paul VI initiated a reorganisation of all curial departments, with a view to making them more international and reflective of changing balances within the modern Church.

SACRAMENT

From the Greek word for 'mystery'. Sacraments are occasions of grace, sacred actions, instituted by Christ and celebrated in the Church, in which physical, external gestures and words serve as channels of the life of God.

SALVATION

Christian teaching about salvation points to God's deliverance of humanity from sin and death as recorded in Scripture. Other words are used in Christian teaching to describe the same reality of the death and resurrection of Jesus Christ, e.g. atonement, liberation, conversion, and immortality. Salvation is offered to those who believe in the redemptive power of Jesus. The Church teaches that 'the Holy Spirit offers everyone the possibility of sharing the paschal mystery in a manner known to God' (GS2)

SCHOLASTIC THEOLOGY

A term used for Christian theology as developed in the Middle Ages, as a result of the rediscovery and development of classical Greek and Roman culture, especially the thought of Aristotle, by the 'scholastics' or 'schoolmen'. Like all theology it has been described as 'faith seeking understanding;. As the equivalent of 'systematic theology', it may be contrasted with biblical or historical theology.

SECULAR/SECULARISATION/SECULARISM

The Latin word 'saeculum' means 'the world', the temporal order. It is frequently thought of as equal to 'profane' and is contrasted with 'sacred'. 'Secularisation' was originally used to describe the confiscation of Church property by the State, against the wishes of the Church. This group of words is now generally used to mean that people treat many things in human life as if they are outside the action of God or a religious sense. Secularism is a recurring phenomenon through the ages, but it has become persistent and widespread only in the modern era and in the western world.

TRENT/TRIDENTINE

Trent is a small town in northern Italy where an ecumenical Council of the Church was held between 1545 and 1563. This Council was concerned with the problems posed by the Reformation. It initiated many reforms and a programme of renewal in the life, liturgy and discipline of the Roman Catholic Church. Tridentine is the adjective from this Council, as in phrases like 'Tridentine reforms', 'Tridentine Mass'.

GENERAL QUESTIONS

1 Discuss the view that, with the calling of Vatican II, a distinctive epoch in Roman Catholic history came to an end.

2 Discuss the influence of the Second Vatican Council on the RC Church in England and Wales.

3 Evaluate the Second Vatican Council's contribution to the reform of ministry and worship in the RC Church.

4 Consider critically the view that Pope John XXIII opened a Council which Pope Paul VI would never have opened, and that Pope Paul VI concluded a Council that Pope John XXIII could never have successfully directed.

5 The four Constitutions have been described as 'the key to unlock the teaching of Vatican II'. Do you agree?

6 Many people regard the Second Vatican Council as a blessing for the Catholic Church, while some regard it as a disaster. Why? What do you think?

7 Do you agree with the view that the post-conciliar Church has not lived up to its promise?

8 In your opinion, does the post-Vatican II Church help or hinder a solution to the problems of Northern Ireland?

9 Assess the contribution of the Second Vatican Council to the search for Christian Unity.

10 Show how the call for an educated adult Church is explicit and implicit in the documents of Vatican II.

11 Discuss critically the role of ministry and authority in the Roman Catholic Church in England and Wales in the period 1850 to the present day.

12 Discuss the relationship between relevant documents of Vatican II and the ARCIC agreements.

13 To what extent does Vatican II offer women a changed role within the Church?

14 What problems for the movement towards Christian unity are presented by the Anglican Church's decision to ordain women?

15 Evaluate Vatican II's understanding of the relationship between the Church and the world.

16 Evaluate the history of Jewish-Christian dialogue this century in the light of Vatican II and the Israeli-Vatican exchange of diplomatic representatives.

17 Evaluate Vatican II's understanding of the modern world, with particular reference to Justice and Peace issues.

18 Assess critically the development of the papacy in the period 1846 to the present day.

19 Assess developments in Religious Education in Great Britain from 1870 to the present day.

QUESTIONS ON DOCUMENTS

20 'Vatican III's statement on the nature of Revelation represents a decisive development in the Church's doctrine.' Do you agree?

21 Comment on the view of some that 'the liturgical reforms introduced by Vatican II were too few, too late.'

22 To what extent is Vatican II's teaching on the nature of the Church a development of previous tradition?

23 Elucidate the place of lay Catholics in the Church according to the teaching of the Second Vatican Council.

24 How does Vatican II understand the Church's missionary activity?

25 Do you agree that Vatican II's teaching on non-Christian religions marked a turning point in the Church's relations with other faiths?

26 Discuss the view that Vatican II marked a radical change in the Catholic understanding of Religious Freedom.

BIBLIOGRAPHY

A DOCUMENTS AND COMMENTARIES

Ed. Norman P Tanner, SJ, *Decrees of the Ecumenical Councils, vol. 2*, Sheed and Ward and Georgetown University Press, 1990. (The translation used in this book.)

Ed. Walter M. Abbott, SJ, *The Documents of Vatican II*, Geoffrey Chapman, 1966. (The first standard collection of Council documents.)

Ed. Herbert Vorgrimler, *Commentary on the Documents of Vatican II*, 5 volumes, Burns and Oates, Herder and Herder, 1967f. (Very scholarly. Useful for high-flyers, but not easy.)

Adrian Hastings, *A Concise Guide to the Documents of the Second Vatican Council*, 2 volumes, Darton, Longman and Todd, 1968/69. (A very good basic commentary, worth searching for in libraries.)

Ed. Austin Flannery, OP, *Vatican Council II: the Conciliar and Post-conciliar Documents*, Dominican Publications, Dublin, 1975. (Another standard collection of texts from or following Vatican II.)

Ed. Austin Flannery, OP, *Vatican Council II: More Post-conciliar Documents*, Dominican Publications, Dublin, 1982. (Sequel to the above.)

English translations of individual Council documents and other papal texts (e.g. encyclicals) are published by Catholic Truth Society, London.

Simplifications of major Council Documents and other papal texts were prepared by the members of Grail and published by Geoffrey Chapman in the late 1960s and 1970s.

B. STUDIES OF THE THEOLOGY OF VATICAN II

Leon J, Cardinal Suenens, *Coresponsibility in the Church*, Burns and Oates, Herder and Herder, 1968.

Leon J, Cardinal Suenens, *Memories and Hopes*, Veritas, Dublin, 1992. (An enlightening insider's view of Vatican II's distinctive theology, as it developed during the Council.)

Christopher Butler, *The Theology of Vatican II*, revised and enlarged edition, Darton, Longman and Todd, 1981.

George Basil, Cardinal Hume, *Towards a Civilisation of Love: Being Church in Today's World*, Hodder and Stoughton, 1988.

Avery Dulles, *The Reshaping of Catholicism*, Harper and Row, San Francisco, 1988.

C. THE SIGNIFICANCE OF VATICAN II- MEMOIRS, BOOKS AND SOME DEVELOPMENTS

Xavier Rynne, *Letters from Vatican City* (and three further titles), London, 1963-66. (A journalist's account of the four sessions.)

Edward Schillebeeckx, *Vatican II: a Struggle of Minds*, Gill and Son, Dublin, 1964.

Michael Winter, *Whatever Happened to Vatican II?* Sheed and Ward, 1985.

Edward Schillebeeckx, *Vatican II: the Real Achievement*, Sheed and Ward, 1967.

John Moorman, *Vatican Observed*, Darton, Longman and Todd, 1967. (A view of Vatican II by an Anglican bishop who was an official observer at the Council.)

Ed. Alberic Stacpoole, *Vatican II by those who were there*, Geoffrey Chapman, London, 1986. (A collection of twenty-three essays by participants in Vatican II.)

Ed. Adrian Hastings, *Modern Catholicism: Vatican II and After*, SPCK, London, 1991. (Essays on various aspects of the thought and influence of Vatican II by various commentators.)

The Easter People - this message of the Bishops of England and Wales issued in the light of the National Pastoral Congress remains a valuable source for appreciating 'what came next' in the context of these countries.
Issued with series of discussion booklets, St Paul Publications, 1980.

Joseph Dunn, *No Lions in the Hierarchy*, Columba Press, Dublin, 1994. (Controversial, stimulating essays on personalities and issues in the post-Vatican church by a priest who has made many documentary films for Irish television.)

D BIOGRAPHIES (JOHN XXIII & PAUL VI)

Peter Hebblethwaite, *John XXIII: Pope of the Council*, Geoffrey Chapman, 1984 (1994).

Peter Hebblethwaite, *Paul VI, the First Modern Pope*, HarperCollins, 1993 (1994).